THE INTERNATIONAL CHEESE RECIPE BOOK

BY
EVOR PARRY

VENTURA BOOKS
New York City
Printed in the United States
All Rights Reserved

Ventura Associates, Inc.
200 Madison Avenue/New York, 10016

INTRODUCTION

No one knows how cheese was discovered or who discovered it. One thing, however, is for certain; wherever humankind has herded milk-producing animals, they have made cheese. It is thought that cheese originated in the Far East; in fact, it is mentioned throughout the Old Testament. Cheese then traveled from the Near East to Europe. The Romans introduced it to the English Isles. The Pilgrims brought it with them when they colonized the Americas.

Literature and history are dotted with references to cheese. Shakespeare makes references to it in his sonnets. Boccaccio satirizes the village of Parmesian in *The Decamaron*. France erected a statue to Madame Harel, who invented Camembert and spread it throughout the French Empire.

The Swiss have been making their cheese since the 16th Century. They eat more cheese than any other people on earth.

Monks near the caves of Roquefort started producing world famous blue-veined cheese around 1070 A.D. It is still very much in demand, domestic imitators, price and availability not withstanding.

Since cheese is a milk product, most experts feel that herders experimenting with ways to deal with surplus milk came up with cheese. Cheese stores longer, unlike highly perishable milk, and in fact gets better with aging, in many instances. England's famous Stiltons and Cheddars are prime examples.

Americans, who consume approximately 2 to 3 million pounds of cheese a year, know that it is a high protein food. With 6 to 12 grams of protein each ounce, depending on the type of cheese, it is highly competitive with other foods. Cheese is such a popular American food that its consumption has risen over 47% in the last ten years. Few Americans, however, actually know how cheese is produced.

Fifty years ago, it was not uncommon for each farm family to produce its own cheese. Farmers knew that whole milk could be coagulated by the addition of a substance called rennet, which is commonly found in the digestive tracts of herd animals. Quite simply, with the addition of this substance, the milk is divided into two parts: the curd and the whey. Whey is the remaining milk liquid. Curd is the semi-solid substance we call cheese.

The curd can be left fresh and be made into cheeses such as ricotta and cream cheese, or be aged. Aged cheeses are said to be fermented. Fermented cheeses are easily divided into two categories: soft cheeses such as Camembert, and harder ones such as Cheddar. The difference in cheeses amount to the curiosities of their makers. Obviously, people like Madame Harel were not content with the already discovered types of cheese and went on to establish their own varieties. Camembert cheese is so beloved by the French people that Madame Harel is a person of honor in her native Normandy village.

Until the early 1900's, American cheese-making was largely focused on the rich dairylands of upstate New York. The bulk of New York Cheddar was produced on individual farms. In 1851, however, the first cheese factory opened in America. By the mid-1900's, Wisconsin had taken over as the largest mass-producer of cheese for the nation, an honor it still holds. Today, however, cheese is produced in every state in the nation.

Although there are thousands of variations from state to state, and in different nations, most experts agree that there are only 18 to 20 basic types of cheese. Among the most popular are:

* Cheddar. Perhaps everyone's favorite cheese, cheddar originated in the village of Cheddar, England. It has a sharp, tangy flavor, dependent on the length of the aging process. Very sharp cheddar crumbles and grates easily. The milder types, sometimes referred to as Cheshire or American (both slight variations) are perfect sandwich cheeses.

* Cream Cheese. This fresh, unfermented cheese can be eaten with virtually anything. The mild taste and soft texture make it ideal as a base for spreads, frosting, crusts, and dips.

* Swiss. Its pierced body, pleasing, pliable texture and nutty flavor have made this cheese a world favorite. Aged or imported Swiss cheeses may have a stronger flavor, but all are extremely adaptable to a variety of cooking needs.

* Cottage Cheese. Everyone's favorite diet food, cottage cheese is a highly versatile food. This fresh, unfermented cheese is usually made of skim milk and blends easily into a variety of recipes, or stands equally well on its own.

* Parmesan. Like cheddar, Parmesan is named after the Italian village whom supposedly originated it. When not fully aged, it makes a great sliced food. Most Parmesan, however, is fully aged and grated. It tops many cooked dishes and makes wonderful sauces.

* Roquefort. By using only ewes milk and curing their cheese in the surrounding caves of the Roquefort area, the monks who originated this cheese centuries ago managed to create a perrenial favorite. It is distinguished by the distinct blue veining of the cheese's body and its pungent, sharp taste.

* Camembert. Its status as Napoleon's favorite cheese with its runny texture and distinctive, high

flavor helped to boost the popularity of this great French cheese. It should always be served at room temperature to highlight its runny quality.

* Edam. A bright, red rind is the hallmark of this mild, flavorful, Dutch cheese. Served at room temperature, it is easily spreadable.

* Provalone. Italy's distinguished, round or pear-shaped cheese is highly adaptable to a varied usage because of its subtle, smokey taste.

Obviously, these are not all the cheeses available or everyone's favorites. Americans do, however, consume a large amount of the aforementioned types. Cheese is certainly becoming as important a food in America as it has long been in Europe.

The history and usage of cheese is intricately tied to the development and needs of humankind. The highly storeable nature of cheese, its vast range of flavors, its nutritional value, and a large variety of cooking uses have strengthened its position as a world food source. In this book, I have endeavored to arrange and compile an assortment of flavorable and interesting recipes involving an array of great cheeses. This should only be your beginning, though. Many of these recipes can stand the test of improvisation. If you have a favorite dish or cheese, experiment. The addition of cheese to almost any of your ordinary dishes will only improve the flavor.

Table of Contents

VI. Main Courses

VIII. Breads, Muffins and Pastries

VIII. Desserts

IX. Sauces and Frostings

Soups

Vegetable-Cheese Soup

1 cup grated Swiss cheese
1 small, shredded head of cabbage
1 large potato, sliced
1 Qt. milk
3 T. butter
pinch of salt, pepper

Cook the shredded cabbage and potato together until soft in lightly salted, boiling water. Drain. Mash together with a large fork and add milk, butter, salt and pepper. Cook over a low flame for 10-12 minutes. Remove and dish into bowls. Spoon in grated Swiss. Place under broiler for two minutes or until slight crust forms.

Vegetable-Cheese Soup II

¼ cup mixed grated Romano and Parmesan
10 oz. beef broth
1 lb. can of cooked tomatoes
9 oz. cooked green beans
1¼ cups water
1 T cornstarch
½ cup cooked spinach
2 T butter
½ cup cooked broccoli
1 mashed clove of garlic
½ cup diced onions, raw

Brown the onions and garlic in butter. Mix water and cornstarch and place them in a large pan with the broth and shredded tomatoes. Add the onion and garlic, along with the other vegetables and most of the cheese. Heat. Transfer to a serving bowl and sprinkle with the remaining cheese. Serve.

Creamy Cheese Soup

2 oz. finely grated Cheshire cheese (or any mild, white cheese)
1¾ pints milk
1 cup croutons
1 large, diced, white onion
2 T butter
2 oz. flour
salt and pepper to taste
a pinch of white pepper
2 egg yolks
2½ oz. double cream
4 T cooked peas

Place the chopped onion in a pan, cover with water and bring to a boil. Drain. Melt one tablespoon of the butter in a pan and add the onion. Saute', covered for about 4 minutes. Put aside and place the remaining butter in the pan and stir in the flour. Next, blend in the milk, salt, pepper and white pepper, bringing the mixture to a boil. Then allow the mixture to simmer for 6 to 8 minutes and strain.

Return soup to the pan, stirring in the cream, egg yolks, and the cheese. Heat slowly to ensure evenness of the mixture. Do not boil. Garnish with cooked peas and croutons.

Cheese Dumplings

1 cup grated Edam cheese
1 egg
1 cup fine-crumbed soda crackers
⅛ tsp salt
⅛ tsp pepper
1 tsp chopped parsley

To the lightly beaten egg, add seasonings, cheese, and enough crumbs to form a mixture that keeps its shape. Half-teaspoonfuls of the mixture dropped into any boiling soup will form dumplings. This recipe makes 24 dumplings.

Quick Cheddar-Shrimp Soup (for six)

1 cup finely grated Cheddar
2 cups heated milk
1 onion, chopped
4 medium potatoes, diced
1 cup heated half and half
2 T butter
¾ cup boiling water
1/3 cup diced celery
¼ cup sherry
1/3 cup chopped chives
1 tsp salt

¼ tsp black pepper
1 lb. fresh cooked shrimp

Place the onion and celery in a skillet with butter and saute' until tender. Transfer to a larger pan, and add the potatoes, boiling water, salt and pepper. Cover and allow to simmer. Leave covered for twenty minutes until the potatoes are done. Slowly, add the milk, shrimp, and half and half. Raise heat, stirring constantly and slowly add the cheese. When the cheese is melted, add sherry, stir, reduce heat and serve. Garnish with chopped chives.

Italian Cheese Soup

2½ cups grated Edam cheese
5 slices of thin black bread
5 cups chicken consomme'
2 T butter
sliced Provolone cheese
sliced Cheddar cheese

Heat the consomme', bringing to a boil, and then letting it simmer. Fry the slices of bread in a buttered skillet. Poach the eggs in the consomme, drain them and place the eggs over the fried bread in the heated bowls. Pour the consomme over the eggs and sprinkle with generous amounts of Edam cheese. Serve with slices of Provolone and Cheddar cheese.

Cheesey Onion Soup

2 cups coarsely grated Swiss and Provolone mixture
3 large peeled onions
5 cups of beef bouillon
1 T butter, sweet
1 T white flour
salt and pepper to taste
5 crusty slices of French bread

Slice the onions into thin rounds and brown them in a saucepan with the butter. Slowly stir in the flour and salt and pepper. Transfer about 4 tablespoons of the bouillon to the saucepan to loosen all ingredients, and then pour everything into the bouillon. Bring to a boil and let simmer for 15 to 20 minutes. Dry toast the five slices of bread in the oven lightly. Place the bread in warm bowls and pour the soup over it. Spread generous amounts of cheese over the top and brown under the broiler. Serve.

Salads

Salmon-Cheese Mousse

2 cups of creamed Cottage cheese
2 cups heavy cream
2 egg whites
2 egg yolks
2 pkgs plain gelatin
2 T fresh lemon juice
6 T melted butter
1 lemon peel, grated
1½ cups crumbled Zwieback crackers
1 can of salmon
½ cup milk
½ cup cold water
½ tsp salt
½ tsp nutmeg

To form the crust, place the melted butter, crumbs and nutmeg into a bowl and mix. Using about ¾ of the mixture, coat the sides and bottom of a 7½ inch baking pan which you've pre-buttered. Set aside.

Gelatin should be softened in a saucepan of cold water. In another pan, mix the milk, salt and egg yolks. Stir constantly over a low flame until thickened. The egg mixture should coat your spoon. Remove, stir in the gelatin and set aside.

Beat the Cottage cheese with the lemon peel, juice, and egg mixture until smooth. Flake the salmon and fold it in.

Beat the egg whites until stiff and fold them into the mixture. Whip the cream and fold it in. Spoon mixture over crust and sprinkle with remaining crumbs. Chill for four hours before serving.

Blue Cheese Mold with Crab

¼ lb. crumbled Blue cheese
2 cans crab meat
3 shredded carrots   1 tsp grated onion
1 cup grated cucumbers   2 T minced pimentos
¼ cup fresh lemon juice   4 T minced parsley
1 cup heavy cream   1 T minced caper
1 cup boiling water   a dash of salt
   a pinch of white pepper

With the lemon juice, soften the gelatin for 4-6 minutes. Combine this with boiling water, stir and set aside.

Blend the Blue cheese with parsley, capers, cucumber, pimento and onions. Season to taste. Stir in the gelatin and refrigerate. Watch the mixture closely. When it begins to gel, remove it. Whip the cream with a chilled beater in a chilled bowl and then fold it into the gelatin.

Coat any 6-inch ring mold with oil and pour the mixture into it. Refrigerate for 4 to 5 hours.

Mix the crab and shredded carrots. After unmolding the ring, fill the center with crab and carrot mixture and serve.

Cheese Stuffed Avocado

1 cup grated Baby Gouda
2 avocados
1 can crab meat
1 whole tomato, chopped
½ cup mayonnaise
4 hard boiled eggs
salt and pepper to taste
3 sprigs fresh parsley

Slice the avocados in half and remove the pits. Remove the pulp to a bowl and mix with the Baby

Gouda cheese, the crab, salt and pepper and spoon back into the avocado skins. Garnish with sliced, boiled eggs and fresh parsley.

Cheese Salad

Dressing:
 ¼ tsp dry English mustard
 6 T olive oil
 a dash of black pepper
 2 T vinegar
 ¼ tsp salt

Salad:
 2 cups diced Swiss cheese
 4 diced hard-boiled eggs
 3 slices cooked crumbled bacon
 3 T minced shallots
 5 small, red potatoes
 ½ cup diced celery
 ½ cup mayonnaise
 3 T minced parsley
 a dash of salt and a dash of black pepper

Scrub potatoes, dice and boil in salted water until tender. Drain and sprinkle with dressing lightly. When cool, mix lightly with cheese, onion, most of the parsley, celery, most of the eggs, and the bacon.

Mix mayonnaise with the dressing and pour onto the salad. Sprinkle the remaining egg and parsley on top. Chill for 7 minutes approx. and serve.

Blue-Pear Salad

2 oz. Roquefort cheese
4 ripe pears
4 T cream cheese
½ cup cream
1 oz. butter
pinch salt
paprika

Peel and split the pears, removing the cores. Allow the Roquefort and butter to soften to room temperature and then mix them to a creamy texture. Fill the hollow pears. Mix enough cream into the cream cheese with a light whisk until it will pour, adding a pinch of salt. Place the pears on a bed of lettuce and pour the mixture over them. Sprinkle lightly with the paprika. Chill ½ hour before serving.

Mrs. Smith's Glorified Applesauce

1 cup Cottage cheese
½ cup applesauce
3 T sour cream
1 tsp grated lemon rind
the juice of one lemon
3 T sugar
pulverized nutmeg

Combine the cottage cheese, applesauce, sour cream, rind, lemon juice and sugar in a bowl. Mix thoroughly. Sprinkle with nutmeg and chill for ½ hour before serving.

Four Cheese Chef Salad

¼ cup crumbled Roquefort
½ cup shredded Cheddar
1 head lettuce
1 head endive, curled
4 hard-boiled eggs, sliced
1 cup shredded cooked Turkey
1 cup shredded cooked Ham
salt to taste
½ cup shredded Provolone
1 large scoop small curd Cottage cheese
¼ cup chopped scallions
½ cup chopped carrots
½ cup sliced mushrooms
¼ cup raisins
Freshly ground pepper to taste

Wash and tear the lettuce. Drain and place in a large serving bowl. Chill one hour. Toss lettuce. Place large scoop of Cottage cheese in the middle. Sprinkle shredded meats around. Crumble Roquefort and sprinkle it on. Add raisins, carrots, mushrooms and onions. Top with Provolone and Cheddar cheese. Add a dash of salt and pepper and serve.

Edam Salad

Dressing:
6 T half and half
1 T fresh squeezed lemon juice
¼ tsp tarragon
a dash of salt

½ cup Sour Cream
1 T French mustard
¼ tsp basil
a dash of paprika

Salad:
  One head of lettuce, torn into pieces
  ¾ cup of shredded roast beef
  ¾ cup of coarsely shredded Edam cheese
  2 hard boiled eggs, crumbled

   Make the dressing first. Combine all ingredients and chill for twenty minutes.
   Toss lettuce, roast beef, Edam cheese and ¾ of the eggs and place on serving plates. Pour on the dressing and sprinkle with the remaining egg.

Mrs. Smith's Cheddar and Grape Salad

1 cup cubed sharp Cheddar cheese
½ cup Sour Cream
2 cups seedless green grapes
honey
¼ cup cream
½ cup Cream Cheese

   Allow cream cheese, cream and honey to reach room temperature. Thin sour cream with the cream slightly. Pour in the honey to sweeten according to taste. Toss the grapes and cheese with this mixture. Transfer to a glass bowl and chill for one hour. Serve.

Special Swiss Salad

½ lb. Baby Swiss cut into thin strips
Bibb lettuce
leaf lettuce Endive
½ cup shredded carrots
½ cup French dressing

Wash lettuce and tear into small pieces. Chill for at least an hour.

Marinate the sliced cheese in French dressing for 1 to 2 hours. Drain. Toss the lettuce in a bowl with the carrots and then place the cheese on top. Chill and serve.

Gruyere and Lobster Cooler

¼ lb. thinly sliced Gruyere cheese
2 cups cooked, cold Lobster
1 head of lettuce
½ cup French dressing
capers
2 whole tomatoes, wedged

Slice the cheese and lobster into cubes and mix well with French dressing. Pour into a bed of crisp, chilled lettuce. Garnish with capers and tomato wedges.

Cheese Mousse

2¾ oz. finely grated Camembert cheese
2½ oz. finely grated Roquefort cheese
1 beaten egg yolk
1 envelope gelatin
¼ cup cold water
1 T sherry
1 tsp. Worcestershire sauce
1 beaten egg white
½ cup whipping cream

Sprinkle the gelatin into the ¼ cup cold water and set aside to soften. Dissolve completely over steam. Place both cheese, egg yolk, sherry and Worcestershire in a blender, and work at medium speed until smooth. Add gelatin and blend again. While these ingredients are being blended, allow a mixing bowl and an egg beater to chill in your refrigerator. Use them to whip the egg whites until fluffy, and then beat the whipping cream to the same texture. Fold both into the cheese mixture. Place into a mold and chill until firm.

Sandwiches
&
Savories

If you still think of the cheese sandwich as a slab of Swiss on white with mayo, take a look at these imaginative suggestions.

Cheddar Dogs

Spread Dijon mustard on two slices of Rye bread. Slice two hot dogs lengthwise, having pre-cooked them in boiling water. Top with diced onions, thinly sliced tomatoes and shredded Cheddar cheese. Place under a hot broiler for 3 to 5 minutes and serve.

Hot Cheese Sandwiches

2½ cups shredded Gouda cheese
4 slices rye bread
4 slices of ham
4 slices raw onion
4 slices tomato
salt and pepper to taste
a dash of paprika
butter

Toast the bread slightly and butter it. Lay it, butter side up, on a cookie sheet. Place the ham, then onion, then tomato on each slice. Cover each generously with Gouda. Season. Place under broiler for 5-7 minutes to slightly melt the cheese. Sprinkle with paprika.

Baked Tuna Sandwich

2 cups Muenster and Cheddar cheese, mixed
3 beaten eggs
8 slices rye bread
1 cup tuna
1½ cups milk
¾ tsp salt
mustard
8 slices cooked, crumbled bacon
3 T mayonnaise
⅛ tsp black pepper
¼ cup celery, chopped
2 T minced onion
2 T minced green pepper

Mix the tuna, celery, bacon, onions, mayonnaise, peppers and black pepper together. Butter a baking dish and set aside. Spread the bread with mustard and pile with tuna. Top with cheese, using only half. Cover with remaining bread and sprinkle on cheese. Beat the eggs, milk and salt together, and pour over sandwiches. Bake a 325° for 35 to 45 minutes, or until cheese puffs and browns.

Cheese Toasties

1 cup finely grated Parmesán
8 slices pumpernickel bread
wedges of sharp Cheddar cheese
1 cup milk
2 beaten eggs
½ tsp salt
a dash of black pepper
Apricot peach jam

Mix the beaten eggs, milk and Parmesan cheese

with the seasonings. Dip the pumpernickel bread into the mixture and fry in butter until brown. Turn and brown the other side. Serve with apricot or peach jam and wedges of sharp, crumbly Cheddar cheese.

Cucumber Sandwiches

Filling:
  8 oz. softened Cream cheese
  1 grated cucumber, unpeeled
  ½ tsp chopped onion
  a generous dash each of onion, salt and fresh ground
   black pepper.
Topping:
  3 oz. Cream cheese
  ½ T orange juice
  ½ tsp grated orange peel
  6 slices extra thin white bread, trimmed of crust

Mix all the ingredients of the filling. Blend until smooth. Chill for 15 minutes.

Mix the topping and blend until creamy. Chill for 5 to 10 minutes.

Lay the two pieces of the trimmed bread out. Spread with filling. Top with another slice and repeat. Cut each into thirds and spread with topping. Chill for 10 minutes before serving.

Stuffed Sausage

¾ lb. shredded American cheese
12 slices fried, drained, and crumbled bacon
12 Polish sausage Franks
12 Hot-dog buns, toasted and buttered
1 T mustard
½ cup pickle relish

Slit the sausages three quarters of the way through lengthwise. Set aside. In a bowl, mix the relish and mustard. Blend in the cheese. Blend in the bacon. Stuff each sausage with the mixture. Secure with toothpicks. Broil the sausage till done, then place in buns.

Muenster Savory

2 cups coarsely shredded Muenster cheese
2 T butter, melted
1 T minced onion
1 egg, hard-boiled
1 T flour
2 T fresh lemon juice
12 slices cooked bacon
2 T chopped green olives stuffed with pimento
2 drops tabasco
⅛ tsp salt
½ cup cream

Saute' the onion with the butter over a low flame. Do not brown. Stir in the flour and allow the mixture to bubble. Remove from the flame. Add the salt, tabasco and cream. Stir constantly. Return to the heat and to a boil. Allow to boil 2 minutes. Remove and add the lemon juice. Mix the olives and the cheese mixture. Sprinkle with crumpled bacon and broil on hot for 4 minutes.

Jumbo Sandwich

Make three slices of the cheesey French Toast. Drain. On the bottom slice, pile shredded ham and a slice of Swiss cheese. Place on another slice of French Toast. Spread toast with Dijon mustard and shredded chicken. Lay a slice of Swiss cheese on top, then a slice of tomato and some lettuce. Top with the last slice of toast. Slice diagonally and pin with toothpicks to secure.

Cheddar Surprise Sandwich

On a thick slice of French bread, spread a thin layer of chili sauce. Put down a layer of diced onions and thin sliced frankfurter rounds, pre-cooked. Put down a layer of baked beans, sprinkle with diced green olives and layers of shredded, sharp Cheddar cheese. Broil for 5 minutes. Serve.

Onion Savory

4 oz. finely grated Edam cheese
2 T minced scallions
¼ cup sweet butter, softened
½ tsp Worcestershire sauce
¼ tsp garlic salt
a dash of white pepper
12 slices of black bread, toasted and trimmed of crusts

Again, allow cheese and butter to reach room temperature and blend until smooth. Add spices, onion and Worcestershire sauce. Mix well and set aside.

Roll the toasted, trimmed bread lightly with a rolling pin. Spread each piece with cheese mixture, roll and secure with toothpicks. Broil 1-3 minutes. Garnish with sliced olives and serve.

Finger Luncheon Sandwiches

4 medium slices of Gouda cheese
2 whole eggs
1/3 cup cream
3 T butter
¼ tsp salt
a dash of paprika
8 slices white bread, trimmed of crusts
Hot mustard

Beat the eggs in a bowl, mixing in the cream and salt. Set aside. Spread the trimmed bread with butter and mustard. Place the cheese slices on the bread and cover with the remaining slices. Heat the butter in a skillet. Dip the sandwiches in the egg mixture and fry on a low flame until browned on both sides. Drain, mat, and serve.

Cheddar Savory

4 oz. finely shredded sharp English Cheddar cheese
2 T mayonnaise
¼ cup softened sweet butter

1 rsp fresh lemon juice
¼ tsp garlic salt
1 tsp French mustard
a dash of white pepper
12 slices toasted, cracked wheat bread, trimmed of crusts

Allow cheese and butter to reach room temperature and then blend until smooth. Next, add pepper, salt, mayonnaise and lemon juice and blend until thoroughly mixed. Set mixture aside.

With a rolling pin, lightly roll the trimmed toast to make it flexible. Spread each piece with cheese mixture, roll in the shape of a tube and secure with toothpicks. Broil for 1-3 minutes and serve.

Liverwurst and Cheese Sandwich

On toasted black bread, spread a thick coating of liverwurst. Sprinkle with a dash of horseradish and a slice of Swiss cheese. Put a slice of raw onion on, cover with another slice of black bread spread with English mustard and grill in a buttered heated skillet until heated through.

Mozzarella Savory

2 T finely grated Parmesian cheese
1 cup coarsely shredded Mozzarella cheese
½ cup diced pitted green olives
½ stick sweet butter
6 slices black bread
½ clove pressed garlic
a dash of freshly ground black pepper

Toast and butter the black bread and set it aside. In

a bowl, mix the olives, both cheeses and the garlic. Spread the mixture generously on each slice of bread, and top with pepper. In a hot broiler, broil for one minute and serve.

An American Hero

Slice a small hero lengthwise and butter it. Cover both sides with sandwich ham, slices of Swiss cheese, American cheese and pickle loaf. Place thin slices of tomato and coat with Parmesan. Broil for 3-5 minutes.

Another American Hero

On a small hero cut in half lengthwise, arrange slices of cooked bacon and tomato. Sprinkle generous amounts of coarsely shredded American cheese and sprinkle with freshly ground black pepper. Broil for 4 to 5 minutes and garnish with thick dill slices.

Three-Cheese Grill

On Rye bread, spread with butter, place a slice of raw onion, Provolone, Cheddar and Muenster cheese. Season with garlic, salt and black pepper. Lay down a slice of tomato and spread the top piece of rye with regular mustard before grilling in a hot buttered skillet.

Hors D'Oeuvres Dips & Spreads

Camembert Hors D'Oeuvres

3 oz. softened Cream cheese
4 oz. Camembert cheese, grated
2 T softened butter
¾ cup milk
1 beaten egg
½ cup finely crumbled bread crumbs
¼ cup all-purpose flour
¼ tsp salt
⅛ tsp Worcestershire sauce
2 tsp water
4-6 drops tabasco sauce

Both cheeses must be forced through a food mill and blended until smooth. Add the flour, milk, salt, butter, Worcestershire and tabasco sauce. Blend. Place over a low flame and stir mixture until thick and smooth. Let cool, cover and refrigerate for at least eight hours. After chilling, roll cheese mixture into small balls and dunk in bread crumbs and egg and water mixture. Deep fat fry for 1 minute. Drain, dry and insert toothpicks. Place on a platter and serve.

Pecan Log

6 oz. softened Cream cheese
1 cup finely chopped pecans
1½ tsp chili powder
2 cloves pressed garlic
4 drops tabasco sauce
⅛ tsp Worcestershire sauce
⅛ tsp salt
⅛ tsp black pepper

In a bowl, blend the Cream cheese, salt, tabasco and

Worcestershire sauce. Add the pecan and garlic and mix well. With your hands, shape the mixture into a roll 4 or 5 inches long.

On a sheet of waxed paper, evenly spread out the chili powder. Roll the log in the powder. Wrap in plastic and refrigerate for 5 hours before serving.

Crisp Cheese Snacks

3 cups Cheddar cheese grated
3 cups fine, sifted white flour
2 tsp vegetable oil
1 tsp salt
¼ cup corn starch
4-5 sprigs fresh parsley, chopped
4 T melted butter
¾ cups cold water

Using a fork, mix salt, water, flour and oil into a dough ball. Dampen a square of folded cheese cloth, cover, and let stand for approximately an hour. Roll the dough and cut into 4 pieces, then roll each piece as thin as possible. Sprinkle the grated Cheddar on each of the four sections and sprinkle with parsley. Then fold each section closed, pinching the edges closed and cutting into four more strips. Place in a buttered baking dish and cover with melted butter. Bake at 350° for 25 minutes or until brown.

Stuffed Celery (Two Versions)

1 stalk of celery, washed and separated into pieces

A) Filling:

1 cup crumbled Blue cheese
1 T butter
4 T finely chopped almonds
1 T finely chopped parsley

Let cheese and butter soften to room temperature, then mix to a creamy texture. Mix in almonds, then spread on the celery. Sprinkle parsley on top and chill before serving.

B) Filling:

3 oz. Cream cheese
2 T cream
1 T chopped parsley
1 T minced chives

Again, soften cheese. Blend in cream, chives and parsley. Spoon onto celery and chill until serving time.

Snack Balls

½ cup finely grated Provolone cheese
14½ cubes of Cheddar cheese
2 cups cooked rice
1 beaten egg
1 cup crumbled bread crumbs
1 T melted butter
1 tsp salt
a generous dash of pepper
2 tsp French mustard

Place rice and grated cheese in a bowl and mix. Pack

a ball of the mixture around each cube of cheese. Dip first in the beaten egg, then bread crumbs, and then deep-fat fry for 7 minutes.

Liptauer, American-Style

8 oz. Cream cheese, softened
1 small onion diced
2 finely chopped anchovy fillets
1 tsp capers
1 tsp paprika
3 T sour cream
1 T French mustard
½ cup sweet butter, softened
1 tsp caraway seeds
¼ tsp salt

Mix the softened cream cheese, sour cream and butter together in a bowl. Blend well. Mix in the anchovies and onion and all other ingredients. Beat until creamy smooth. Transfer to serving bowl and chill. Garnish with fresh parsley. This makes an excellent spread for black bread and crackers.

Cheese Cocktail Pleasures

½ oz. grated New York sharp Cheddar cheese
¼ cup sweet butter
1 cup sifted white flour
¾ tsp paprika
¼ tsp white pepper

Allow the grated Cheddar to warm overnight in a covered container. Sift together the flour, paprika and white pepper. Set aside. Mix the softened butter with the Cheddar, then mix in the dry ingredients.

With a pastry and star tube (No. 7), squeeze out 2 in. lengths on a greased cookie sheet. Bake at 375° for 12 minutes.

Puffs

1 jar of American sharp Cheese spread
4 oz. softened Cream cheese
2 eggs
½ cup flour
½ cup water
¼ cup butter
¼ tsp salt

Mix the water, butter and salt in a saucepan, slowly bringing the mixture to a boil. Add flour. Stir constantly until mixture forms a ball shape, leaving the sides of the pan clear. Remove from the heat, blending in both eggs, one at a time. Beat the mixture until a smooth, even texture is achieved. Stir in both cheeses, blending well. Use a teaspoon to dollop dough onto a greased cookie sheet. Bake at 400° until golden brown. Serve.

Cheesey-Clam Dip

6 oz. Cream cheese
10 oz. canned drained clams
1 sliver of garlic, crushed
1 T fresh lemon juice
1 tsp Worcestershire sauce

½ tsp salt
⅛ black pepper

Place all ingredients except clams in a blender. Cover and blend at a high speed for one minute. Add clams and blend at a medium speed until smooth. Chill 30 minutes and serve.

Curried Olive Spread

1 cup shredded mild Cheddar cheese
2 oz. sour cream
6 oz. Cream cheese
½ cup sliced green olives
1 T chopped chives
2 T sherry
¼ tsp salt
½ tsp curry powder
¼ cup chopped celery
chutney

Mix the Cheddar, Cream cheese and sour cream (all softened to room temperature) with the chutney, curry, sherry and salt. Mix in the sliced green olives and blend all until creamy smooth. Transfer to a bowl and sprinkle with chopped chives. This makes an excellent sandwich spread on an hors d'oeuvres with fresh vegetables and crackers to dip.

Croquettes

½ cup grated Gouda cheese
6 large mashed potatoes
2 whole eggs
1 cup fine bread crumbs
¼ tsp pepper

½ tsp salt
½ cup of milk

Combine the cheese, potatoes, eggs and seasonings. With your hands, work them into balls. Dip them in milk, then in the bread crumbs, and deep fry. Serve as appetizers with wedges of Cheddar cheese and sliced apples.

Beefy Cheese Ball

2 cups finely grated sharp Cheddar cheese
8 oz. softened Cream cheese
¾ cup pickled relish
approx. 12 oz. of shredded corned beef
1½ tsp French mustard
2 tsp horseradish
3 T lemon juice
½ tsp grated lemon peel
½ tsp Worcestershire sauce
½ cup finely ground fresh parsley
1 cup ground walnuts

Mix the cheeses, corned beef, relish, mustard, lemon juice, rind, horseradish and Worcestershire sauce in a large bowl with a mixer or a blender. Mix thoroughly. With your hands, shape the mixture into a ball and cover with foil. Refrigerate for at least two hours. About 30 minutes before serving, remove and roll in parsley and ground nuts.

Fried Gruyere

8 slices of Gruyere
1 cup fine, dry bread crumbs
1 whole egg
½ cup milk

½ tsp salt
⅛ tsp black pepper
¼ stick butter

Combine the egg, milk, salt and pepper. Dip the cheese in the mixture and then into the bread crumbs. Repeat. Heat the butter in a skillet and fry the dipped cheese until brown.

Home-made Port Cheese Spread

½ cup crumbled Roquefort cheese
1¼ cups finely grated sharp Cheddar cheese
5 T Cream Port

Place all ingredients in a bowl and beat together until creamy. Place in a tightly covered container and refrigerate for 24 hours before serving. Makes about 1¼ cups of spread. Excellent on black bread.

Deviled-Cheese Dip

6 oz. Cream cheese
2½ oz. deviled cheese
1 sliver crushed garlic
1 T fresh lemon juice
½ cup mayonnaise
½ tsp salt
⅛ tsp black pepper

Place all ingredients in the blender, cover and blend until smooth. Chill for 30 minutes and serve.

Blue-Cheddar Party Dip

2 T Roquefort cheese
2 cups finely grated Cheddar
4 T milk
½ cup mayonnaise
2 T French mustard
2 tsp horseradish

Place Cheddar and Roquefort in a bowl and blend until smooth. Keep blending, adding mayonnaise, horseradish and mustard. Next, start adding milk while you blend until you achieve a desired consistancy. Serve with Taco chips, celery, crackers, and carrots.

Mexican Party Dip

6 oz. softened Cream cheese
1 can condensed black bean soup
2/3 cup chopped, pitted black olives
2 tsp fresh lemon juice
1 tsp grated lemon rind

Place Cream cheese, lemon juice and rind into a mixing bowl and beat until fluffy. Add the black bean soup slowly and mix thoroughly. Add the olives and mix and mix. Chill for 30 minutes and serve with Taco chips.

Cream Cheese Olive Spread

3 oz. Cream cheese
1/3 cup sliced green olive with pimentos
2 T cream
¼ cup diced celery
1 drop tabasco
a pinch of salt

Allow the Cream cheese to reach room temperature. Beat the softened Cream cheese until fluffy. Add the cream and seasonings. Blend.

Mix in the olives and celery. Makes an excellent spread for sandwiches, crackers or vegetables.

Quick Cheese Dip

3 oz. Cream cheese
¼ lb. crumbled Cream cheese
¼ cup sour cream
½ diced onion
2 T pineapple juice
2 tsp Worcestershire sauce

Into an electric blender, place all the ingredients. Blend at a medium speed until smooth. Chill for 30 minutes and serve.

Cottage Spread

1 cup small-curd Cottage cheese
4 slices of fried, drained, crumbled bacon
2 tsp mayonnaise
½ tsp grated onion
2 T chopped gerken
a pinch of paprika

Cream the Cottage cheese and mayonnaise together and blend with the bacon. Lightly mix the gerken, paprika and onion in with the mixture. Chill.

Green Cottage Cheese Dip

1 cup creamed, small curd Cottage cheese
1 large peeled diced, pitted ripe avocado
1 pressed clove of garlic
2 tsp minced onions
2 tsp fresh lemon juice
3 T chopped parsley
½ tsp salt
¼ tsp black pepper
a dash paprika

Begin by creaming the Cottage cheese in a bowl until smooth. In a separate bowl, smash the ripe avocado with the lemon juice. Blend the avocado and Cottage cheese together thoroughly and the remaining ingredients except paprika. Blend until smooth. Place in a bowl, sprinkle lightly with paprika. Chill and serve.

Cheddary Olive Drops

1 cup grated sharp Cheddar cheese
3 T melted butter
3 T minced onion
2 dozen whole pitted olives
½ cup flour
1 tsp millk
⅛ tsp salt
⅛ tsp dry English mustard
a drop of tabasco

In a bowl, mix the cheese and a sifted mixture of the flour, salt and mustard. Slowly add the butter, milk and tabasco to form a doughnut-like texture. Set aside. Stuff the olives with the onions and roll them into balls of dough. Drop onto a greased cookie sheet and bake for 10 minutes at 425°

Zippy Dip

1/3 cup crumbled Roquefort cheese
3 cups finely grated Cheddar cheese
1 T softened butter
¾ beer
1½ tsp grated onion
2 drops tabasco
¾ tsp dry English mustard
½ tsp Worcestershire sauce

Allow the cheese to reach room temperature. Mix Cheddar and Roquefort together. Blend until smooth. Add slowly the beer, butter, onion, mustard, tabasco and Worcestershire sauce. Blend until smooth. Chill in a covered container for 2 to 3 hours. Serve.

Side Dishes

Marie's Cheese Potatoes

½ cup shredded Edam cheese
6 medium baking potatoes
5 T butter
½ cup heated cream
8 slices cooked, crumbled bacon
1 T chopped onion
½ tsp salt
¼ tsp paprika
¼ tsp freshly ground pepper

Before baking the potatoes, rub the skins with a tablespoon of butter. Bake for an hour. Mash the potatoes and discard the skins. Mix in the rest of the butter and heated cream and seasonings. Whip. Mix in the cheese, bacon and onion. Place in heated, buttered baking dish. Dust lightly with paprika and bake at 425° for 10 more minutes.

Cheddar-Tomato-Olive
Potatoes

Follow the recipe for *Marie's Cheese Potatoes*, but substitute sharp Cheddar for the Edam. When you add the bacon and onion, mix in one cup of diced green olives and a half cup of diced tomatoes, drained.

Traditional Kugel

7½ oz. un-salted Farmer's cheese
3 beaten eggs
½ cup sugar
the juice of one lemon
the grated peel from one lemon
1½ cups natural applesauce
½ cup diced, dried apricot
½ lb. thin noodles
1 cup sour cream
1 T melted butter
¾ tsp salt

Cook the noodles, drain and rinse in very cold water. Set aside.

Mix the cheese, eggs, applesauce, sugar, peel, lemon juice, apricots, salt butter. Mix well. Gently, fold the noodles into this mixture. Add the sour cream and blend well.

Place mixture into a greased baking dish and put into 350° oven for 50 minutes. Remove, let cook, slice and serve.

Brussel Sprouts Stuffed
With Cream Cheese

4 oz. Cream Cheese
1 lb. brussel sprouts
1 T fresh cream
1 T finely grated horseradish
¼ tsp salt
¼ tsp pepper

Boil the Brussel Sprouts for 4-5 minutes in lightly

salted water. Drain. Mix the Cream cheese, salt, pepper, and horseradish with the cream to form a paste and stuff between the leaves of the Brussel Sprouts. Chill for 40-50 minutes and serve.

Ham and Swiss Custards (for 4)

½ cup grated Swiss cheese
1½ cups shredded cooked ham
2 slightly beaten eggs
¾ cup scalded milk
a pinch of black pepper

Combine the ham and cheese in a bowl. Set aside. Slowly stir the scalded milk into the eggs, and then pour over the ham and cheese mixture. Mix thoroughly. Pour the recipe into 4 buttered custard cups. Place the cups in a shallow pan of water and bake for 35 minutes, till brown. Serve.

Cheese Fritters

1½ oz. Parmesian finely grated
2 egg whites
2 T heavy cream
¾ lb. boiled potatoes
pinch of salt
pinch of black pepper
pinch of white pepper
large pinch finely chopped parsley
2 egg yolks

Boil the potatoes, drain and keep hot. Whip the egg

yolks with the cream and mix the potatoes, cheese and various seasonings. Beat the egg whites and fold them into the mixture. Drop one tablespoon at a time into a deep-fat fryer and fry until golden brown and crispy.

Cheese-Stuffed Tomatoes

1 cup finely grated Colby cheese
4 large tomatoes
4 T heavy cream
1 whole egg
1 tsp chopped parsley
½ tsp salt
¼ cup crumbled bread crumbs
a dash of black pepper

Wash and scoop out centers of the tomatoes. Retain the cap. Season. Combine the cheese, cream, eggs and parsley in a bowl and mix. Fill the tomatoes and sprinkle in bread crumbs. Replace the caps and place in a buttered baking pan. Bake at 325° for 17 minutes. Serve.

Cheese Pesto (for Pasta)

6 tsp finely grated Parmesan cheese
2 tsp dried basil
3 cloves minced garlic
1/3 cup un-salted butter
3 oz. Cream cheese
3 oz. Blue cheese
1 bunch finely chopped parsley
¾ cup olive oil
dash of salt and pepper

Allow Cream cheese, butter and Blue cheese to reach room temperature. Mash the basil, garlic, and parsley into them. While mashing, slowly add the olive oil. Next, stir in the Parmesan, salt and pepper. Cover and refrigerate until ready to serve, tossed with hot pasta.

Peppery Cheese Loaf

8 oz. grated Cheddar cheese
2½ cups milk
2 whole onions
2 cups cubed, stale bread
1 bay leaf
2 cloves
2 eggs
a dash of nutmeg
generous, fresh-ground black pepper

Pour the milk into a mixing bowl, placing the onions, bay leaf and cloves in with it for approximately 12 minutes. Do not heat. Butter or oil a souffle' dish and alternate layers of Cheddar and bread cubes, peppering each layer of cheese generously according to taste. Top with a layer of cheese. Retrieve onions, cloves and bay leaf from the milk and dispose of them. Beat the two eggs and stir them into the milk along with the nutmeg. Pour the mixture over the cheese and bread cubes and bake for 30 minutes in a 350° oven.

Scalloped Mushrooms

½ lb thin sliced mild Cheddar
1 cup sliced mushrooms
1 cup cream
2 eggs, whole
6 slices of white bread, trimmed
2 T butter
½ tsp salt
½ tsp paprika
a generous dash of freshly ground black pepper

In a buttered casserole, arrange three slices of bread, then mushrooms, then cheese. Repeat. Dot with butter. In a bowl, mix cream, eggs and seasonings. Beat. Pour over casserole. Bake 35 minutes at 325°.

Cheese Knishes

Cheese Filling:
  ½ lb Farmers cheese
  ½ lb Cream cheese
  2 T butter, not salted
  1 T sour cream
  1 egg
  1 onion, diced
  a pinch of sugar

Knish Dough:
  2 beaten eggs
  ½ lb melted butter
  2½ cups white flour
  ¼ cup warm water
  2 T dry yeast
  ¼ cup sugar
  ½ tsp salt

Make the dough first. Begin by dissolving the yeast in warm water and setting it aside. In another bowl, beat eggs and mix in the butter, sugar, and salt. Mix in the dissolved yeast.

Slowly add the flour while mixing thoroughly.

Cover the bowl with a damp cloth and refrigerate for two hours.

Roll out half of the dough at a time and then cut it with a 4-inch cookie cutter.

Filling: Saute' the onions in butter until tender, but *do not* let them brown. Mix onions with sour cream, both cheeses, sugar, egg and any remaining butter. Mix until slightly smooth. Spoon out a generous tablespoon of cheese filling on a dough round, place another on top and crimp the edges. Bake at 350° for 22-26 minutes on a greased cookie sheet until brown.

Baked Cheese and Spinach

1 cup grated Swiss and Parmesan mixture
2 lbs cooked spinach
¼ cup heated olive oil
dash salt, black pepper, nutmeg

Butter a baking dish and arrange alternating layers of cheese, spinach and olive oil. Season the layers with salt, pepper and nutmeg. Bake at 325° for 15 minutes.

Baked Cheese and Tomatoes

3 oz. grated Gruyere and Parmesan cheese
1 lb. tomatoes, skinned
3 chopped shallots
4 T bread crumbs
2 oz. butter
salt and pepper to taste

Cut the tomatoes in half, salt and pepper them and

place in a shallow baking dish. Cover them with chopped shallots. Mix the cheese and bread crumbs together and spoon onto the tomatoes. Next pour a little of the melted cheese over each and bake in a preheated, 375° oven for 10-12 minutes.

Lima Surprise

1 cup crumbled Roquefort cheese
1½ cups cooked lima beans
¼ cup bouillon stock
2 T bread crumbs
2 tsp butter
a pinch of black pepper

Into a buttered baking dish, alternate layers of lima beans and Roquefort cheese. Your final layers should be beans. Pour bouillon stock over and sprinkle with bread crumbs and pepper. Dollop with butter. Bake at 350° until top turns crisp.

Cheese-Stuffed Peppers

1 cup grated Swiss cheese
2 cups cooked rice
¼ cup chopped celery
¼ cup chopped pimento
½ cup chili sauce
½ cup smashed bread crumbs
8 T butter
8 green peppers, uniform in size
salt to taste

Remove the pepper stem and seed the peppers.

Parboil in lightly salted water for five minutes. Drain. Melt 4 tablespoons of butter in a large skillet and saute the celery until tender. Add chili sauce, pimento, cooked rice, some salt and the grated Swiss. Next, fill parboiled peppers with the mixture. Top off with bread crumbs and the remaining (melted) butter. Peppers should then be placed in a baking dish containing ½-inch of hot water. Bake at 350° for ½ hour.

Asparagus Parmigana

10 stalks of fresh, steamed asparagus
4 T finely grated Parmesan
2 T melted butter
a generous dash of freshly ground black pepper

After removing the asparagus from the steamer, lay the stalks on a heated oblong serving dish. Sprinkle with cheese and butter and place in a pre-heated 400° oven for 5-7 minutes. Remove and serve.

Green Beans Au Gratin

1 lb fresh green beans
¾ cup shredded Cheddar cheese
¾ sour cream
1 chopped onion
2 T butter
2 T flour
2 T water
2 T lemon juice

1 tsp salt
½ tsp pepper
½ cup bread crumbs, crumbled

Steam green beans over lightly salted water until al

dente. Set aside. Melt butter in a larger skillet and saute onions until brown. Slowly add flour, water, salt, pepper and lemon juice. Let simmer 3 to 4 minutes. Stir in the beans and sour cream. Mix thoroughly. Place the mixture in a buttered casserole and top with Cheddar cheese and bread crumbs. Bake at 350° for ½ hour.

Cheese Rice

1 cup grated Cheshire cheese
1 cup milk
water
1 cup rice
½ cup bread crumbs
½ stick butter
dash of salt
dash of black pepper

Cook rice in water for 17 minutes and drain. Pour in the milk and cook for the remaining 10-12 minutes. In a buttered baking dish, lay down layers of rice, butter dollops, salt, pepper and cheese. Cover the top with bread crumbs and bake at 350° for approximately 15-20 minutes.

Cheese Broccoli Italian Style

1 cup grated Parmesan cheese
1 large bunch fresh broccoli
1 clove garlic
1 small onion, diced

2 T olive oil
4 T butter
pinch of salt

Steam the fresh broccoli over lightly until al dente. Remove from the steamer and trim the stems leaving only the flowerettes. Put aside. In a large skillet, heat the olive oil, butter, sliced onion and sliced clove of garlic. Saute garlic until brown and then remove. Place the broccoli in the skillet, sauteing lightly for 10-12 minutes. Remove and place in flame resistant cooking dish. Sprinkle Parmesian cheese over the broccoli and place under broiler until the cheese melts. Serve.

Twice Baked Potatoes

1 cup finely grated Cheddar cheese
4 large potatoes, baked
6 T cream
1 can Deviled ham
½ tsp salt
dash of black pepper
¼ cup melted butter

Cut the baked potatoes in half. Delicately, scoop out the insides, leaving the skins whole. Mix the potatoes with the cheese, egg, deviled ham and seasonings. Mix in the cream until fluffy. Scoop the mixture back into the skins and bake in a 350° oven for 12-17 minutes. Serve.

Cheese Potatoes

2 cups grated Gruyere cheese
3 beaten eggs   1½ tsp salt
6 potatoes   ¼ tsp pepper
2 T butter   1½ cups scalded milk
1 diced onion   dash of paprika

Sauté the diced onion in a shallow pan until tender. Drain. Scrub potatoes and slice them thin. Put potatoes in a mixing bowl with the beaten eggs, scalded milk, salt, pepper, half the grated cheese and sauteed onion. Mix. Pour the mixture into a large greased baking dish. Spread the rest of the Gruyere cheese on top and sprinkle with paprika. Bake in a preheated oven at 350° for one hour until the top is golden brown.

Green Beans and Samsoe

4 oz. grated Baby Samsoe cheese
2 lbs. fresh green beans
¼ cup melted, sweet butter
a generous dash paprika
pinch of salt

Trim and clean the green beans. Place in a covered pot with 1 cup cold water and salt. Boil. When the water boils, reduce heat to a simmer and let sit for 20 minutes.

In a double boiler, melt the Baby Samsoe cheese. Remove the beans to a heated serving plate and cover with melted butter, then the melted Samsoe cheese, and last, the paprika. Serve.

Cheese Potatoes

1 cup shredded Provolone cheese
¾ cup warmed milk
¼ cup softened butter
½ cup chopped onion
6 potatoes, peeled, diced, cooked and drained
½ tsp salt
¼ tsp black pepper

In a saucepan, melt the butter and saute' the onion. Whip the cooked potatoes in a bowl, slowly adding the warmed milk. Mix in the butter, onions. Provolone and seasonings. Serve in a warmed bowl.

Swiss Potatoes

1 cup grated Swiss cheese
3 T butter
1 pint light cream
2 lbs peeled, sliced, potatoes
3 crushed cloves garlic
dash pepper
dash salt

Butter a baking dish and line it with the potato slices. Add seasonings.

Heat the cream just to the point of boiling. Pour over the potatoes. Add butter. Bake in a pre-heated oven between 1½-2 hours at 350°. Remove.

Pour the grated Swiss over the casserole and return to the oven. Adjust heat to 400°. Bake for 10-12 more minutes and serve.

Main Courses

Coquilles St. Jacques (for 4)

½ cup grated Swiss cheese
1 cup cream
1 lb fresh scallops
2 cups water
the juice of one lemon
2 egg yolks
3 T butter
2 T sherry
2 T white flour
1 bay leaf
1 tsp salt
¼ tsp black pepper
dash of paprika

Wash the scallops, place them in a bowl and sprinkle evenly with lemon juice. Allow them to simmer in water with the bay leaf and one tablespoon of butter for five minutes. Drain and set aside.

Melt the other two tablespoons of butter in a sauce pan. After removing from the heat, blend in the flour, salt and pepper, and slowly blend in the cream until the mixture is smooth. Next, beat in the eggs and cheese over the low flame and cook for three more minutes. Add the sherry and the scallops, stir and pour into a buttered baking dish. Bake at 350° for 20 minutes.

Cheese-Stuffed Burgers

1½ cups mixture of Edam, Cheddar, and Romano cheese, finely grated
1 lb ground beef
¼ tsp pepper
1 tsp salt
a few drops of Worcestershire sauce

In a bowl, mix the ground beef, salt, pepper and Worcestershire sauce. Roll into eight patties. Top four of the patties with the cheese mixture and top them with the other four patties. Seal the edges tightly and broil.

Beef Parmigana

¼ cup finely grated Parmesan cheese
4 slices of American cheese
4 slices of Mozarella cheese
8 slices of thin roast beef
1 beaten egg
1/3 cup fine bread crumbs
¼ cup butter
¾ cup tomato paste
2 T milk
1 tsp salt
⅛ tsp black pepper

Mix the egg, pepper, salt and milk together. Heat the butter in a skillet. Dip the roast beef into the egg mixture and let soak. Mix the Parmesan and crumbs together. Remove the beef and dip in the crumbs. Brown in the butter over a low flame. Drain. Cover the beef with the two remaining cheeses and top with tomato paste. Over a low flame, cook 20 more minutes.

Veal Parmigana

½ cup freshly grated Parmesan cheese
3 oz. sliced Mozzarella cheese
2 beaten eggs
2 lbs boneless veal cutlets
2 cans tomato sauce
1¼ cups crumbled bread crumbs
¼ lb fresh sliced mushrooms
1 T water
1 tsp salt
1/3 cup olive oil
¼ tsp pepper
½ tsp rosemary

With a meat hammer, pound the veal until it is extremely thin and then cut it into six equal pieces.

Heat the olive oil and saute the mushrooms. Remove from the oil.

Mix together the Parmesan and the bread crumbs. Place the water, eggs, salt and pepper in a bowl and mix well.

Dip the veal first in the egg mix and then the bread crumbs. Brown the cutlets in the olive oil and then add the tomato sauce, mushrooms and sliced mozzarella over the veal. Reduce heat, cover and allow to simmer 7-10 minutes. Remove and serve.

Cannelloni

Dough:
- 2 large eggs
- 2 cups white flour
- ¾ tsp salt
- 1½ T warm water

Filling:
- ¼ cup shredded Parmesan
- ¼ lb softened Cream cheese
- ½ lb ground beef
- ¼ cup minced, fresh parsley
- 2 crushed cloves garlic
- 1 pint Ricotta cheese
- ½ lb ground veal
- ¼ cup olive oil
- ½ tsp basil
- dash of salt, dash pepper

Sauce: Mornay Sauce (see Mornay Sauce)

Begin with the dough. Begin mixing the eggs, flour and salt in a bowl with your fingers. Add water until dough can be rolled into a ball. Knead until stiff and divide into thirds. Roll each third very thin and cut into 3¼ inch squares. Throw six or seven at a time in a gallon of salted boiling water for 4-6 minutes. Drain and set aside.

Heat the olive oil and brown the meat. Drain all fat and allow meat to cool. In a bowl, thoroughly mix the meat with all the other ingredients to form a filling. Place 2 tablespoons of filling on each 3½ inch square of dough and roll tightly closed. Place the cannelloni in a buttered shallow dish and cover with Mornay sauce and Parmesan. Bake at 365° for 17 minutes.

Cheesey Eggs Florentine

2 oz. grated Cheddar
¾ cup milk
1¼ oz. flour
2 oz. butter
6 eggs
1½ lbs fresh spinach
salt and pepper to taste
dash of dry mustard
1 tsp vinegar

Poach the eggs in water with about 1 tsp vinegar. The water should simmer on a low heat and not boil. Poach the eggs 3-4 minutes, remove from the water and place in cold water until needed.

Boil the spinach and drain the pan. Add ½ oz. of butter and salt and pepper. Remove and arrange spinach in a baking dish. Prepare the Mornay sauce. Slowly bring to a boil the remaining butter, flour, milk, mustard and seasonings, before adding the cheese. Place the eggs on the spinach and cover with sauce. Bake in a 400° oven for 10 minutes, uncovered.

Greek Casserole

½ cup finely grated Parmesan cheese
¼ cup finely grated Romano cheese
2 lbs ground beef
¼ cup tomato sauce
1 large chopped white onion
6 T butter
1/3 cup tomato paste
1 beaten egg

1 lb macaroni, cooked
1 cup bread crumbs
½ cup white wine
¼ cup melted butter
¼ cup fine bread crumbs
½ tsp pepper
¼ tsp cinnamon
½ tsp nutmeg
1½ tsp salt
1 tomato diced

Brown the beef and onions in butter. Slowly, add the tomato paste, wine, spices and diced tomatoes. Simmer for 10 minutes, let cool and mix in the egg and fine bread crumbs.

Butter a large casserole. Cover the bottom with bread crumbs. Put in half the macaroni and cover it with about ¼ cup of the Parmesan and Romano mixed. Top the cheese with the beef. Add more cheese and cover with the remaining macaroni. Top with tomato sauce and the last ¼ cup of cheese and the remaining bread crumbs. Pour on melted butter. Bake for ½ hour at 400°.

Cheesy Potato Pancake

3 ox. grated sharp Cheddar
8 potatoes, skinned and sliced an ⅛ inch thickness
2 T butter
dash salt, pepper

Melt the butter in a large skillet and arrange the first layer of potatoes so that they cover the skillet, overlapping. Next, season lightly and add a layer of cheese. Repeat. End with a layer of cheese. Cover the pan and cook at a medium heat for 40-50 minutes. Loosen and serve. Garnish with orange and apple slices.

Eggs Ricotta

1 cup Ricotta cheese
1 dozen hard-boiled eggs
½ tsp dry English mustard
2 T chopped scallions
salt and pepper to taste
garnish with watercress and a dash of paprika

Shell the hard-boiled eggs and cut down the center lengthwise. Remove the yolks. Place yolks, ricotta, salt and pepper in a bowl and mash together. Scoop the mixture into the egg whites, garnish with paprika and watercress. Serve chilled.

Marie's Meat Loaf

1½ cups Ricotta cheese
½ cup finely grated Parmesan cheese
2 eggs, beaten
½ lb ground sausage
1 lb ground round
¼ cup chopped onion
1 T chopped chives
1 cup mashed bread crumbs
2 T chopped fresh parsley
½ cup milk
1 tsp salt
⅛ tsp freshly ground black pepper

Mix the beef, sausage, one egg, salt, pepper, bread crumbs, Parmesan, onion and parsley lightly together in a bowl. Divide into two parts, packing one half into a greased baking dish. In another bowl, mix the chives, the other egg, and the Ricotta. Pour over meat. Fill with remaining meat mixture. Bake 80-90 minutes at 350°.

Cheese Waffles

2 oz. grated Cheddar cheese.
2 eggs
3 oz. melted butter
8 oz. white flour
1¼ cup buttermilk
1 tsp bicarbonate of soda
2 tsp baking powder
generous pinch of salt

Sift the flour, bicarbonate of soda, baking powder and salt into a bowl. Make a well in the center of the mixture and add the eggs and melted butter there. Mix. Begin adding the buttermilk with a whisk, until smooth. Next, fold in the cheese. When it is mixed, spoon onto a preheated waffle iron. Serve with butter.

*Other types of cheese, such as any sharps, may be substituted.

24 Swiss Pancakes

1½ cups grated Swiss cheese
3 beaten egg yolks
¾ cup sour cream
2 T white flour
½ tsp salt
½ tsp dry English mustard
a generous dash of Thyme
2½ T butter

One at a time, add the beaten egg yolks and sour cream to the cheese. Mix the flour and seasonings together. Mix well. Add to the cheese mixture and mix well. Melt the butter in a large skillet and drop the batter in to form pancakes. Flip to brown.

Cheddar Pancakes with Ham

Follow the Swiss Pancakes recipe, however, substitute 1½ cups grated, sharp Cheddar for the Swiss cheese. After mixing all the other ingredients, fold in shredded cooked ham, about ¾ cup. Drop the batter into a hot buttered skillet. Brown on both sides. Serve with butter and maple syrup.

24 Swiss Pancakes with Walnuts

Follow the Swiss Pancake recipe. After mixing all other ingredients, fold in diced walnuts and drop batter into a heated, buttered skillet. Brown pancakes on both sides. Serve with strawberry jam.

Cheese Kabobs

Stuffed olives filling:
  5 oz. tangy cheese spread
  9 oz. ripe olives, pitted and left whole
  2 tsp horseradish
  1 tsp French mustard
  3 drops of tabasco
  ⅛ tsp salt

Drain the olives and set aside. In a bowl, mix the cheese and seasonings. With a small spoon, scoop the cheese filling into the olives and allow to chill slightly.

Set out bowls of shrimp, wedges of tomatoes, sections of green pepper, small onions and cubed, marinated chunks of beef (pre-browned), whatever your favorites are. Skewer the olives and the other fixings. Place the kabobs on the broiler rack under a hot broil, and cook, turning frequently for 4-7 minutes. Serve hot.

Noodles with Parmesan and Cottage Cheese

5 oz. container of Cottage cheese
2 oz. grated Parmesan
4 oz. white flour
2 egg yolks
2 oz. butter
½ tsp salt
1 T oil
fresh black pepper to taste

Mix the Cottage cheese, egg yolks, flour and salt in

a bowl and mix with a wooden spoon, forming the mixture into the shape of a ball. Cover with a damp cloth and let stand an hour. Roll out about an ⅛ inch thick and cut into strips. Add the oil and a pinch of salt to boiling water and then throw the noodles in. Let boil for 6 minutes, drain and place in a heated bowl. Stir the Parmesan, butter and fresh pepper over them. Serve.

Eggplant/Cauliflower Casserole

1½ cups sharp Cheddar cheese, shredded coarsely
1 eggplant, peeled, cubed and bled
1 cauliflower (just the flowerets)
¼ cup minced onion
2 beaten egg yolks
3 T butter
¼ cup melted butter
1 cup bread cubes
a dash of black pepper
1 2/3 cups evaporated milk
1 T fresh lemon juice
½ cup water
3 T flour
½ tsp salt

Steam the cauliflower and eggplant until just barely tender. Set aside. Heat the butter in a skillet and toss with the bread crumbs until brown. Set aside.

Place the melted butter in the top of a double boiler. Heat and add the flour, onion, salt and pepper. When it bubbles, remove from the flame. Stir in the milk and water and return to the heat. Stir rapidly and allow to thicken. Remove a little of the sauce and mix well with the beaten egg yolks. Pour into the sauce and mix well. Let simmer for 5 minutes while stirring. Add the Parmesian and lemon juice. Blend. Pour over the eggplant and cauliflower in a buttered baking dish. Place in a 350° oven for 30 minutes.

Large Feta Lamb Pie

1½ cups crumbled Feta cheese
3 cups cubed, roast lamb
1 cup diced cooked potatoes
4 hard-boiled sliced eggs
the juice from two lemons
½ cup olive oil
1 T grated lemon peel
1 beaten egg
4 cups cooked rice
1 cup boullion
24 filo (pastry) leaves
½ stick melted butter
2 T fresh mint
2 T fresh parsley
1 tsp salt
½ tsp oregano

Use half of the lemon juice to sprinkle the lamb, then set aside. Butter a two inch deep 14 x 10 baking pan and line it with 12 of the Filo leaves. Put one leaf down at a time and spread each one with the melted butter.

Top the filo with the layer of rice mixed with all the other ingredients, including the lamb.

Lay down another layer of filo leaves using the same method as the bottom layer. Bake at 250° for approximately 2 hours. Serve.

Swiss Fondue For Two

2 cups shredded Swiss cheese
2 T light brandy
1 cup white Riesling wine
1½ T white flour
1 clove garlic
a dash of salt, black pepper and nutmeg
a loaf of crusty bread, cubed
2 tart red apples, cubed

Mix the cheese and flour. Rub the fondue pot with the garlic clove and then remove it. Pour in the wine and set the flame on low, letting the wine heat, but not boil. While stirring the heated wine with a fork, begin *slowly* adding the cheese and flour mixture, making sure each amount added is thoroughly dissolved before adding another. When the mixture bubbles slightly, add the seasonings. Last but not least, add the brandy and continue stirring. Remove, and put on a low flame on the alcohol fire. You may now dip the bread and fruit into the mixture.

Gruyere Olive Tart

½ lb thin sliced Gruyere cheese
½ cup finely grated Parmesan
shortcrust pastry
¼ cup milk
4 egg yolks
½ cup pitted diced green olives
2 T butter
a dash of salt

Your baking dish should first be lined with the

pastry and then be allowed to reach room temperature. Melt most of the batter and brush it on the pastry, then cover it with Gruyere cheese and olives. Mix the egg yolks and milk together to form a custard. Pour it in the pastry over the cheese. Add the pinch of salt. Sprinkle liberally with Parmesan. Bake for 20 minutes in a 325° oven.

Quick Cheesey-Onion Pie (for 4)

½ lb finely shredded American cheese
1½ cups scalded milk
2 whole eggs
1½ cups finely crumbed soda crackers
½ cup melted butter
½ tsp salt
⅛ white pepper

Place the melted butter and the crumbs in a bowl and mix well. Press into an 8 inch pie plate and chill for 5 minutes.

Saute' the onions in butter and then spoon onto the crust. Slowly add the eggs to the scalded milk, and mix. Add the cheese, salt and pepper next. Pour into crust. Bake at 275° for 45 minutes.

Macaroni and Cheese with a Twist

8 oz grated Gruyere cheese	3 eggs
2 T grated Parmesan	salt, pepper and nutmeg
¼ cup smashed bread crumbs	2 tsp butter
1 lb macaroni	1 cup cream

Drop the macaroni in lightly salted water and let cook. Mix the egg yolks, Gruyere, cream, salt, pepper and nutmeg together. Beat. Beat the egg whites and then fold them into the mixture. Drain the macaroni and add it. Spread butter and bread crumbs into a souffle dish and then spoon in mixture. Place the dish in a larger, shallow dish of water and bake at 325° for 45 minutes. Dollop butter and sprinkle on Parmesan five minutes before the time is up.

Broiled Swiss Flounder

½ cup coarsely shredded Swiss cheese
2 tomatoes, diced
1 lb fillet of flounder
1 stick of butter
1 T grated onion
salt and pepper to taste

The flounder should first be washed and drained. Place the fish in a shallow baking dish that has been pre-buttered. Dot with butter. Season with salt and pepper and then spread the onions and tomatoes over. Place under the broiler at medium heat for approximately twenty minutes. Remove, sprinkle with the shredded Swiss and return to the broiler 5 to 7 minutes. Serve.

Farm Breakfast

½ cup shredded American cheese
5 eggs whole
4 slices lean bacon
1 T onion, chopped
½ tomato, chopped
3 boiled, small potatoes, cubed
½ tsp salt
a generous dash of pepper

Cut the bacon into bits and drain returning about one tablespoon of fat. Add the onions, salt, pepper tomatoes and potatoes. Saute until potatoes start to brown. Add the cheese. Drop in the eggs and stir the mixture. Serve on toast.

English Cheese Surprise

6 T grated Cheshire cheese
4 egg whites
4 egg yolks
2 oz. of butter
2 T flour
2 T cream
½ cup milk
pinch of salt

Heat the butter in a pan, adding the milk, cream and flour slowly until you've achieved a sauce. Remove from the heat and mix in ¾ of the Cheshire cheese, egg yolks, and salt. Next, fold in the egg white and steam in a cooking dish for an hour. Remove from steam, cover with remaining cheese and bake for 12-16 minutes until brown. Serve.

Marinated Blue Cheese Steak

¼ cup finely crumbled Blue cheese
1½ lb flank steak
1 small clove of garlic
1/3 cup white wine vinegar
1/3 cup lightly salted water
1½ T soy sauce
Freshly ground pepper to taste

Begin a day before your plan to serve the steak. To marinade the steak, mix the soy sauce, vinegar, water, garlic, onion and pepper in a shallow dish. Score your steak intermittently with a sharp knife and allow to soak uncovered in the refrigerator overnight.

When broiling the steak, begin by grilling on one side for 7-9 minutes and then turning. Spread the Blue cheese on the broiled side, allow the other side to cook, remove and serve.

Feta Stew

½ lb Feta cheese, crumbled into cubes
3 lbs cubed beef
2½ lbs. small white onions, peeled and scored
2 oz tomato paste

1 cup tomato sauce
½ cup red wine
2 T red wine vinegar
1 bay leaf
½ tsp cumin, ground
2 T raisins
a dash of salt
¼ cup olive oil
1 T butter
1 T brown sugar
3 garlic cloves, pressed
8 whole cloves
1 small stick cinnamon
¾ cup diced walnuts
dash of black pepper

Heat the olive oil in a dutch oven, then add the beef and remaining oil. Combine tomato sauce, paste, brown sugar, wine, vinegar, cumin and garlic and pour over the meat. Add the bay leaf, cinnamon and cloves and mix in the raisins. Note: if the bay leaf, cloves and cinnamon are wrapped in cheese cloth first, they'll be easier to retrieve afterwards. Cover and bake it in a pre-heated 350° oven for two hours.

Remove the cheesecloth bag. Stir in the cheese, nuts and whole onion. Remove from the oven and allow to simmer, open, on a stove for 12 minutes. Serve.

Swiss and Crab Casserole

½ cup finely grated Swiss cheese
1 lb cooked crab meat
½ cup dry Rhine wine
1 egg yolk
¼ cup butter

1 cup light cream
3 T flour
½ tsp salt
dash of pepper

Flake the crab meat, and clean. In the melted butter, blend in flour, salt and pepper. Slowly add the cream until smooth and blended evenly. Over a low flame, cook until the sauce is thick and smooth. Next add 2 tablespoons of the sauce to the egg yolk and mix, then add the egg mixture back into the main sauce pan. Continue cooking for about three minutes. Blend the wine and cheese in evenly, and add the crab. Pour the mixture into a buttered baking dish, sprinkle with the remaining cheese and bake in a 425° oven for 7½ minutes. Serve.

Blue Mousse

4 oz Roquefort cheese
7½ oz. double cream
3 T lemon juice
3 T finely chopped parsley
2 T chopped pimento
1 cup grated cucumber
1 tsp finely chopped onion
¼ tsp salt
2 pinches black pepper
6 oz hot water
watercress to garnish
7-inch ring mold
½ oz gelatin

Gelatin should be softened in the lemon juice before the hot water is added to dissolve. Crumble the cheese and mix with the cucumber, parsley, pimento, onion, salt and pepper.

Add the gelatin to this mixture and fold in the slightly whipped cream. Pour into the mold and chill until firm. Garnish with watercress.

Quick Traditional Lasagne

1 pint Ricotta cheese
½ lb sliced Mozzarella cheese
½ lb ground beef
1 lb cooked and drained lasagne noodles
2 cans tomato soup
1 cup diced onion
½ cup water
2 tsp oregano
2 tsp vinegar
2 large cloves crushed garlic

In a skillet, brown the beef, garlic, onions and oregano. Add the water, soup and vinegar and simmer for 25 minutes.

In a large greased baking dish lay down 3 layers of noodles, Ricotta, meat and Mozzarella each. Bake at 250° for 30-35 minutes. Allow to firm for 10 minutes before serving.

Cheddar Souffle'

1 cup coarse, shredded Cheddar cheese
3 T finely grated Parmesan cheese
5 egg whites
1 cup heated milk
¼ tsp dry English mustard
3½ T butter
3 T flour
4 egg yolks
½ tsp salt
¼ tsp Worcestershire sauce

Let egg whites stand one hour, open air, before

whipping. Meanwhile, pre-heat the oven to 400° and use about ½ tablespoon of butter to coat the sides of a 1½ quart souffle dish. Use the Parmesian to sprinkle over the buttered dish sides and bottom.

Melt the remaining 3 tablespoons of butter in a pan over a low flame, adding the flour gradually over the course of 2-3 minutes. Remove the pan, slowly beat in the milk until it is creamy and thick. Next, add the mustard, Worcestershire and salt, returning the pan to the flame briefly until it thickens. Remove from the flame after approximately one minute and beat in the egg yolks. Transfer to a bowl and set aside.

Beat the room temperature egg whites until they stiffen. Add one generous tablespoon to the mixture you just finished and then add most of the Cheddar; stir in well. Next, very gently begin folding the remaining egg whites into the mixture, and then pour the mixture into the prepared souffle dish. Level the top and sprinkle the remaining Cheddar over it. With a spoon, circle through the mixture one inch from the edge and bake. Lower the preheated oven to 375° and bake for 40 minutes. Serve immediately.

Large Cottage Cheese Omelette

1 cup small curd Cottage cheese
3 T butter
6 whole eggs
5 T milk
1 T water
½ tsp salt
a generous dash fresh ground pepper
1 T minced scallions

Beat the eggs, water, seasonings and milk together.

Mix well. Cream the Cottage cheese and blend with scallions. Combine both mixtures. Heat the butter in a skillet. Reduce the heat and pour in the omelette batter. Allow to cook, and fold to form omelette. Serve.

Helen's Meat Loaf

1½ cups finely shredded Mozzarella cheese
½ cup finely grated Parmesan cheese
5 hard-boiled eggs, sliced
2 beaten eggs
1½ lbs ground beef
1½ cups fine cracker crumbs
¼ cup chopped onion
¼ cup half and half
2 tsp salt
¼ tsp black pepper
2 T chopped parsley

Mix the beef, one egg, cracker crumbs, parsley, salt, pepper, milk, Parmesan and onions lightly with a fork into a large bowl. Place half the mixture in the bottom of a greased baking dish. Cover with shredded Mozzarella and sliced eggs. Add the remaining meat and sprinkle with cracker crumbs. Bake for an hour and a half at 350°.

Welsh Rarebit

4 oz sharp grated cheese
1½ T milk
1 T ale   pinch of white pepper
1 tsp mustard   2 T butter
                           hot, buttered toast

Melt the butter in a pan, then add the cheese, moving to a double boiler to melt it into the butter. Stir in the milk, ale, mustard and white pepper. Stir until creamy and then use the mixture to top the hot, buttered toast. Serve.

Italian Macaroni and Cheese

½ cup Parmesan cheese, finely grated
2 cups shredded sharp Cheddar cheese
2 cups white sauce
1 T salt
3 quarts water
2 cups macaroni
¼ cup Cottage cheese
¼ cup tomato paste
¼ tsp. dry English mustard

Heat the water, add salt and bring to a boil. Cook the macaroni and drain. Make a white sauce and thin it with water. Mix the Cheddar cheese, white sauce and the mustard. Mix evenly with the macaroni and pour into a buttered casserole dish. Top with tomato paste, Parmesan and bread crumbs. Bake ½ hour at 350°.

Mexican Macaroni and Cheese

Follow the *Italian Macaroni and Cheese* recipe. Substitute ¼ cup chili sauce for the dry mustard. Leave out the tomato paste.

Cheese Stuffed Pancakes

Pancakes:
- ¼ pint milk
- ¼ pint water
- 2 eggs
- 1 T melted butter
- pinch of salt
- 4 oz. flour

Sift the flour and salt into a bowl and add the eggs. Gradually stir in the milk and water and the melted butter. Beat until thick and smooth. Pancakes are made by pouring the batter into a heated, oiled pan.

Filling:
- 8 oz grated Cheddar cheese
- ½ cup cream
- ¼ tsp paprika
- dash of white pepper

Mix ¼ cup of the cream with most of the cheese and the paprika and pepper. Pour the mixture evenly onto each of the pancakes and roll them. Place in a buttered baking dish. Pour the remaining cream over them and sprinkle with cheese and butter. Place under the broiler for 10 minutes or until brown.

Individual Gruyere and Lobster Casseroles

1½ cups coarsely shredded Gruyere cheese
3 cups diced, cooked lobster meat
2 cups cream
2 T sherry
¼ cup butter
¼ cup flour
⅛ tsp paprika
⅛ tsp crushed nutmeg
½ tsp salt

Heat the butter. Mix in nutmeg, flour, salt and paprika until the mixture bubbles. Remove from the heat and thoroughly mix in the cream. Return pan to the flame. Stir and cook until mixture thickens. Remove from heat and add sherry and lobster. Spoon into the 6 individual casseroles and cover with the Gruyere. Broil at 500° for 5 to 7 minutes.

Baked Blue Chicken

½ lb Blue Cheese, crumbled
1 pint sour cream
2 boneless chicken breasts
4 pressed cloves of garlic
1 cup crumbled crumbs
1 egg beaten

½ cup flour
2 T batter
2 T oil
salt to taste

Salt chicken lightly and then dip in flour. Roll floured chicken breasts in beaten egg and bread crumb mixture. Place oil and butter in a skillet and brown the chicken on both sides.

Place browned breasts in a baking dish and set aside. Mix the crumbled Blue Cheese, sour cream and the garlic. Pour this mixture over the chicken, cover and bake in a 350° oven for 40 to 50 minutes.

Sara's Baked Fondue

3 cups shredded Cheddar cheese
5 slices bread, cubed
2 cups milk, scalded
1 T melted butter
3 T grated onions
1 tsp poppy seeds
4 eggs separated
¼ tsp salt
¼ tsp dry English mustard
¼ tsp black pepper
¼ tsp paprika
1 drop tabasco sauce

Pour the scalded milk into a bowl. Add two cups of the cubed bread, cheese, seasonings and onion. Mix well. Beat the egg yolks and mix them in. Beat the whites until peaked and slowly fold them in. Toss the remaining bread cubes with melted butter and poppy seeds. Pour the mixture into a buttered casserole and top with bread cubes. Place casserole into a shallow baking dish with water. Bake 40-50 minutes at 375°.

Special Eggs for Four

½ lb Colby cheese, thinly sliced
1 small can of tomato soup
10 slices of cooked bacon, crumbled
3 hard-boiled eggs, sliced
4 slices of toasted, unbuttered bread.

Place the Colby in the top of a double boiler and melt. Add the soup and mix thoroughly. Next, add the sliced egg and crumbled bacon; heat well through. Serve on toast.

Cheddary French Toast

1 cup finely grated Cheddar cheese
2 eggs
1/3 cream
8 slices white bread
¼ tsp salt
3 T butter

In a bowl, mix the eggs, cheese, cream and salt. Mix well. Heat the butter in a skillet. Dip the bread into the mixture and fry.

Cream Cheese Pancakes for Four

Filling:
8 oz. Cream cheese
4 T softened sweet butter
¾ cup blueberries
1/3 cup sugar
grated rind from one lemon
2 egg yolks

Batter:
2 cups flour
2 whole eggs
pinch of salt
2 cups milk
Plus: Apple butter and Vegetable oil

Begin with the filling. Allow the Cream cheese to become room temperature. Then blend it in with all the other ingredients except the blueberries. Mix until smooth. Carefully fold the blueberries into the mixture. Set aside. Next, sift the flour and salt into a bowl. Thoroughly mix in one egg and half the milk. Then add the second egg and the rest of the milk. Mix. Cover and set aside for 30 minutes before using.

Oil and heat your pan, turning it as you pour in the batter to form a thin pancake. Flip. Fill each pancake with cream-cheese filling and place on a hot platter. Glaze with apple butter and serve.

Cheddar, Apple, Bacon Waffles

2 cups mild Cheddar grated
½ cup dried apple
¼ cup crumbled fried bacon
1/3 cup melted butter
2 egg whites
2 egg yolks
1½ cups milk
1 T baking powder
1½ T sugar
¾ tsp salt

Melt the butter and set aside. Sift sugar, flour, salt

and baking powder into a bowl and set aside. Beat the egg yolks and milk together. Mix in the butter and cheese. Slowly, mix in the flour mixture until a batter is formed. Beat the egg whites till they peak and fold in the mixture. Fold the apple and bacon in. Drop batter onto a hot waffle iron. Butter and serve with honey and apple butter.

Cheese Stuffed Dogs

2½ inch slices of American cheese
4 hot dogs
4 slices of uncooked bacon
French mustard

Get each slice of cheese into four even pieces. Cut the hot dogs lengthwise ¾ of the way through. Stuff two pieces of cheese in each dog, wrap with a strip of bacon and secure with toothpicks. Cook well away from the broiler for 9 to 12 minutes until the cheese melts.

Baked Eggs and Swiss

½ lb thin sliced Swiss cheese
4 T grated Romano cheese
1/3 cup cream
salt and pepper to taste

Butter a small shallow baking dish and cover the bottom with the sliced Swiss cheese. Break the eggs over the cheese, being careful not to break the yolks. Salt and pepper them and cover with cream. Sprinkle the Romano cheese over the cream and bake in a 350° oven for 17 minutes. Serve.

Roquefort and Eggplant

½ cup crumbled Roquefort cheese
1 large eggplant
1 cup mashed bread crumbs
1 whole beaten egg
2/3 cup grated onion
3 T butter
⅛ tsp mayonnaise
2 T salt

Skin the eggplant and cut into circles. Bleed the eggplant by coating both sides with salt. Leave on for three minutes and then rinse. Pat dry. Dice. Cook the eggplant and onion together until tender, then set aside.

Mix the crumbs, egg, spice and cheese. Toss with the eggplant. Place in a buttered casserole dish. Dot with butter and bake for ½ hour at 350°.

Fettucine Alfredo

¾ cup grated Parmesian cheese
¼ lb sweet butter, twice cubed
½ lb fettucini noodles
¼ cup warm heavy cream
½ tsp. fresh ground black pepper

Cook the fettucine in lightly salted water. Drain. Place the noodles on a hot serving dish. Quickly, add the other ingredients and toss vigorously (as if tossing a salad) until the cheese and the butter melt into a creamy texture. Serve.

Sunday Brunch Recipe

3 cups mild Cheddar cheese
2/3 cup butter
1 cup sliced mushrooms
6 hard-boiled eggs, sliced
¼ cup minced onion
2 T flour
½ cup milk
1¼ cups tomato soup
½ tsp Worcestershire sauce
¼ tsp dry English mustard
¼ tsp salt
a pinch of black pepper

Into a chafing dish, place the butter, mushrooms and onion. Saute'. Remove and set aside. Into the chafing dish mix the flour and seasonings. Heat until bubbling. Remove from the heat and mix in the milk, soup and Worcestershire sauce. Stir and add the cheese, mushrooms and eggs. Return to a low flame and serve.

Tuna and Cheese Casserole (for Six)

¾ lb thinly sliced Swiss cheese
1 large can tuna packed in spring water
2 cups cooked noodles
½ cup bread crumbs
2 T melted butter
2 T finely diced olives
¼ cup grated Parmesan cheese

Flake and drain the tuna. Lay down alternate layers of tuna, noodles and Swiss cheese in a buttered casserole. Cover with olives, bread crumbs, butter and Parmesan cheese. Bake at 350° for 20-30 minutes.

Breads
Muffins
&
Pastries

Cheddar Cheese Bread

2 cups grated Cheddar cheese
2½ cups fine whole wheat flour
3 beaten eggs
1 package active dry yeast
1 T honey
¾ cup warmed milk
¼ tsp salt
¼ cup pure vegetable oil
¼ cup toasted sesame seeds

In a large bowl, mix the warmed milk, eggs, honey and oil. In another bowl, mix in half the flour and add the yeast, salt, cheese and most of the sesame seeds. Mix the contents of both bowls together and beat for 3-4 minutes. Work the rest of the flour into the dough by hand. Let it rise for 1 hour. Place the dough in an oiled loaf pan, and sprinkle the remaining sesame seeds on top. Bake for 45 minutes in a pre-heated 350° oven.

Short Cut Cheese Bread

½ cup sharp grated Cheddar
½ cup grated Parmesan
4 T melted butter
1 loaf unsliced rye bread

Remove all the crust from the unsliced loaf of rye bread except for the bottom crust. Cut lengthwise down the center, to within an inch of the bottom crust. Cut across the width of the loaf every two inches to the same depth. Brush the melted butter onto all exposed surfaces, and sprinkle both cheeses onto the loaf. Bake on a greased sheet in a 525° oven until golden brown.

Cheese Danish Ring

Filling:
  8 oz. whipped Cottage cheese
  11 oz softened Cream cheese
  2 egg yolks
  1 tsp sugar
  ½ tsp vanilla

Frosting:
  2 T cream
  ½ tsp vanilla
  1½ cups confectioner's sugar

Coffee Cake:
  2 whole eggs
  2 egg yolks
  1 cup milk
  1/3 cup sugar
  1½ cups raisins or walnuts
  4 cups flour
  1 pkg. and 1 tsp Active Dry Yeast
  1 tsp salt
  ¼ cup butter

Begin this recipe by making the filling. Combine the Cottage cheese, Cream cheese, egg yolks, sugar, vanilla and cinnamon in a bowl and beat with a mixer until smooth. Set aside. Mix 1¼ cups of flour with the sugar, yeast and salt in a large bowl. Heat a saucepan, melt the butter and heat the milk. Slowly, using an electric mixer, combine milk and the dry ingredients. Beat at a medium speed for about two minutes. Add ¾ cups more flour, along with the whole eggs and one egg yolk. Switch to high speed and beat for two more minutes.

At your own discretion, mix in enough of the additional flour to form a soft dough. Remove to a greased, covered bowl and chill for at least two hours.

When chilled, divide the dough into two sections and roll each out onto a lightly floured board to form a rectangle. Spread the filling evenly on each rectangle and sprinkle with raisins or nuts. Roll up lengthwise and seal. With the sealed edge down arrange it on a greased cookie sheet. Place the other to connect and form a ring. Every 2 inches, snip half-way into the ring with kitchen shears and brush with slightly watered egg yolk.

Let the cake rise for about an hour. *Do not refrigerate.* Meanwhile, mix the confectioner's sugar, cream and vanilla to form a smooth glaze. Bake the coffee cake for 20 minutes at 375° and glaze while still warm.

American Fan Rolls

1 cup grated American cheese
½ stick softened sweet butter
¼ cup melted butter
½ cup pure vegetable shortening
1 T baking powder
1 tsp salt
2 cups sifted white flour

In a bowl, sift the salt, flour and baking powder

together. With a pastry knife, cut in the shortening. Form a well in the mixture and work in the milk with a fork.

Ball the dough and roll on a flour-dusted surface. Knead 12 times. Roll into a ¼ inch thickness and cut it into 5 strips. Spread with butter and sprinkle the strips with cheese. Stack 4 strips and turn the 5th over and stack. Cut into at least 12 equal sections. Brush with the remaining butter and bake for 12 minutes at 450°.

Cheddar Ring

Follow the *American Fan Rolls* recipe, but increase the elements one and a half times. Substitute New York State Sharp Cheddar Cheese for the American Cheese.

After you've made the dough, roll it out ½ inch thick and 7 inches wide. Spread with butter and the grated Cheddar. Roll lengthwise and pinch the edge to seal. Form into a ring and brush with butter. Score the surface and puncture occasionally. Lay on a greased sheet and bake 22 minutes at 400°.

Cheese Shortbread

3 oz. aged Camembert cheese
¼ cup finely grated Swiss
¼ cup butter
3 eggs
2 cups fine flour
1 tsp salt

Let the butter soften to room temperature. Mix butter, Camembert and Swiss cheese together. Beat the three eggs into the mixture, adding the salt and flour. Mix until a soft dough is achieved. Roll out into a circle on a lightly floured board. Cut into wedges and bake in a 425° oven for ½ hour.

Light Cheese Favors

Note: This recipe includes puff-pastry, which requires 8-10 hours of preparation time.

½ cup finely grated Parmesan cheese
1 cup butter
½ & ¼ tsp salt
7 T ice cold water
1 beaten egg white
2 cups white flour
¼ tsp paprika
1 large bowl ½ full of ice cubes

In a bowl of ice cubes, place one cup of butter. While it chills, work, breaking it into small pieces and working in the surrounding ice-water until waxy. Remove, dry and place ¼ cup ır the refrigerator for later use. Roll or pat the remaining butter on a surface, approximately ½ inch thick and divide into fifths. Wrap separately in waxed paper and chill.

In a bowl, sift the flour and salt. With a pastry knife, cut in the ¼ cup butter until the butter is in very small pieces. Slowly mix in the 7 tablespoons, one at a time, and mix lightly. Gather the ball and knead the dough. Place the dough in a covered container and set aside for 20-30 minutes.

Roll the dough out in ¼ inch thickness and into the shape of a sharp rectangle. Cut the remaining pieces of butter into small chunks and cover the center third of the rectangle with it. Fold one side over and one under. Refrigerate for one hour.

Remove the dough and roll out to original-size rectangle. Repeat with the butter and refrigerate for another hour. Repeat three more times. On the last roll-out, fold all four sides toward the center and roll out. Fold in half and wrap. Refrigerate for at least two more hours.

Divide the dough into two equal parts. Roll out half into a rectangle shape and brush the upside with beaten egg white. Sprinkle with paprika, salt and half the Parmesan. Repeat with the other half of the dough.

Cut both into halves, and each half into 1 inch wide strips. Twist and place on a greased baking sheet. Bake for 15 minutes at 400° until golden brown.

Cream Cheese Turnovers

5 oz. Cream cheese
4 thin slices of ham.
5 oz. white flour
6 generous slices of Swiss cheese
1 egg yolk
dash of salt
½ tsp water
dash of pepper
2 oz. butter

Sift the flour and salt together, mixing a little of the

flour into the Cream cheese and softened butter. Slowly add the remaining flour until you are ready to roll out the dough. Roll and cut the dough into three inch squares. On each slice, put a piece of cheese before folding over, pinching the edges together. Place the turnover on a buttered baking sheet and brush them with the egg yolk and water mixture. Bake at 425° for approximately one hour.

Two Dozen No-Work Rolls

1 cup grated Cheshire cheese
2½ cups flour
3 T sweet butter
1 pkg active yeast
1 egg yolk
¾ milk
1 T milk
½ cup water
3 T sugar
1 tsp salt
¼ cup butter, melted

Place the salt, yeast, sugar and about 1½ cups of the flour in a large mixing bowl and blend thoroughly. In a pan, heat ¾ cup of milk, the water and 3 tablespoons of butter. Slowly add the milk mixture to the flour mixture and beat with an electric mixer for 2 to 3 minutes at medium speed. Slowly blend in another cup of flour and beat at high speed for 1 to 2 minutes. Stop beating when sticky dough is formed. Note: it is acceptable to add more flour if needed. The dough should be placed in a greased bowl and covered. Allow to rise for an hour.

Punch the dough. Roll onto a flour dusted surface and divide evenly in two. Take half the dough and roll out into a medium sized rectangle. Brush with melted butter and top with half the cheese. Cut into at least eight sections through the width and cut those sections into thirds and twist. Repeat for the other half of the dough. Place on greased cookie sheets and brush with remaining butter, egg yolk and milk mixture. Let stand for 20-30 minutes and bake for 5-10 minutes at 425°.

Cheese Muffins

1 cup grated American cheese
1 egg
2 cups sifted white flour
3 T melted cooled shortening
3 tsp baking powder
1 cup milk
1 tsp salt

Sift the flour with the baking powder and salt and then mix with ¾ cup of the cheese. Mix the egg shortening and milk together, and then stir into the cheese mixture with a fork. Spoon about 2/3 full into greased muffin pans and sprinkle the remaining cheese on. Bake in 425° oven for 25 minutes until brown.

Monterey Jack-Crab Muffins

4 slices of Monterey Jack cheese
2 English Muffins, separated
½ cup mayonnaise
1 can crab meat, flaked
dash of white pepper

Toast the English Muffins. Mix the crab, mayonnaise and pepper together and spread on the English Muffins. Cover each muffin with a slice of Monterey Jack and brown for a few minutes under the broiler.

Colby Bread

2½ cups shredded Colby cheese
2¼ cups whole milk, scalded
1 pkg. active yeast
2 tsp salt
1 T vegetable shortening
5½ cups white flour
⅛ cup melted butter
¼ cup very hot water
2 T sugar

Soften the yeast in the hot water. Mix the sugar, salt and shortening together. Add scalded milk and beat until smooth. Mix in the yeast. Slowly add the remaining flour, stirring constantly until smooth. Mix in the cheese to form a dough and roll briskly on a flour dusted surface. Set aside for 12 minutes. Roll the dough into a ball and then roll in a greased bowl. Cover and let rise for 45 minutes. Roll the dough on a dusted surface and divide evenly. Let rest for 7 minutes. Punch and place in loaf pans. Brush with butter and let rise for 45 minutes, or until doubled. Bake for an hour at 375°.

24 Indiana Cheese Rolls

1 cup grated mild Cheddar cheese
1 egg white
¼ cup very hot water
1 pkg active yeast
¼ cup vegetable shortening (or more)
1 T fresh lemon juice
1 whole egg
3 cups white flour
¼ cup warm water
½ cup sugar
⅛ cup melted butter
½ tsp salt

Soften the yeast in hot water and set aside. Into a large bowl, pour warm water and mix in ¾ cup of flour. Mix the softened yeast and mix it with the flour until smooth. Cover and let stand in a warmed corner for an hour.

Mix together the grated cheese, lemon juice and shortening until smooth. Add the salt and sugar and cream until fluffy. Beat the egg yolks and slowly add to the mixture. Divide the remaining flour in thirds and mix until smooth and blended into the mixture. Turn the dough onto a flour dusted sheet of waxed paper and allow to rest for 7 minutes approximately.

Knead the dough thoroughly and roll into a ball.

Roll the ball into a greased bowl and cover. Allow to stand for 45 minutes until the dough rises and doubles.

Punch. Knead quickly and allow to rest 7 minutes.

Roll out the dough to a ¼ inch thickness and cut into approximately 3 to 4 inch squares. Fold to form triangles and place on greased cookie sheets. Brush with butter and bake for 40-50 minutes at 350°.

Tangy Cheddar Biscuits

Dough:
    2 cups sifted white flour
    ½ cup vegetable shortening
    ½ cup milk
    1 T baking powder
    1 tsp salt
    6 oz finely grated Cheddar seasoned with garlic powder
    ¼ cup milk, warmed
    ¼ cup melted butter

Begin by sifting together the flour, baking powder and salt. Work with a pastry knife until coarse. Add the shortening and work again. Form a well and add the ½ cup milk all at once. Work until stirrable with a fork.

Roll the dough out to a ¼ inch thickness and about an inch apart on a greased cookie sheet. Place grated Cheddar cheese on half the circles, and cover with the remaining circle of dough. Brush with melted butter and milk. Bake at 450° for 12 minutes. Makes 14 biscuits.

Croutons

These croutons can be used in soups, salads, casseroles or for snacks.

½ cup finely grated Parmesan cheese
1½ cups spoon size shredded wheat
3 T melted butter
pinch of salt, black pepper

To the melted butter, add the shredded wheat and saute for 4-6 minutes. Remove from the flame and gently saute' the shredded wheat with Parmesan. Cover and chill.

Gruyere Strudel

Filling:
  2 cups finely grated Cheddar
  ½ cup heavy cream
  2 T melted butter
  2 beaten eggs

Dough:
  7 T lukewarm water
  ¼ cup melted butter
  2 beaten eggs
  ½ tsp salt

Set aside ⅛ cup melted butter and ⅛ cup heavy cream for basting.

Begin with the filling. Pour all the ingredients into a bowl. Mix well and set aside.

To begin the dough, sift the flour into a bowl.

Slowly mix in the butter, eggs and salt. Add just enough water to allow dough to hold together. Knead for 15 minutes and then set aside for ½ hour.

After 30 minutes, sprinkle a pastry cloth with flour and roll the dough out paper thin. Spread the filling over the dough. Roll the strudel and place it on a baking sheet. Baste with cream and butter. Watch the strudel in its 350° oven, basting frequently. When golden brown, it's finished baking.

Spoon Bread

1½ cups finely grated Cheddar cheese
4 egg whites
4 egg yolks
2 cups scalded milk
1 cup yellow corn meal
¼ cup butter
½ tsp salt
1 tsp sugar

Stirring constantly, slowly mix the scalded milk and corn meal. Stir until thick and smooth. Beat the egg yolks and remove corn meal from the heat. Mix the egg yolks and corn meal mixture. Slowly, blend in the cheese, salt, sugar and butter and beat until smooth. Beat the egg whites till they peak, and fold into the mixture. Turn into a buttered casserole dish and bake for 35-40 minutes in a 375° oven.

Cheese/Date Bread

1 cup grated mild Cheddar cheese
1 beaten egg
1½ cups pitted chopped dates
½ cup milk
1 tsp vanilla extract
¾ cup chopped pecans
3 cups flour, sifted
½ cup sugar
¾ cup hot water
¾ tsp salt
4 tsp baking powder
¼ cup vegetable shortening

Soak the dates in very hot water and allow it to cool. Drain and set aside. Melt the shortening and set it aside to cool. Sift the flour, sugar, salt and baking powder into a bowl. Blend well. Blend the cheese and pecans thoroughly. To the date-water mixture add the shortening, vanilla, egg and milk. Mix well.

Slowly, by forming a well in the dry ingredients, add the date mixture. Mix thoroughly and turn it into a greased loaf pan. Bake at 350° for 60-70 minutes.

Desserts

CHEESE PUDDING

2 cups finely grated Swiss and Parmesan cheese, mixed
1 cup flour
4 eggs separated
¼ cup butter
1 tsp salt
a dash of black pepper

Let butter stand at room temperature until soft. Slowly add egg yolks and beat until creamy. Add cheese, flour, salt and pepper, slowly stirring the butter and cheese mixture. Add the beaten egg whites. Mix well. Spoon mixture into a buttered 8-inch mold with cover. Place the mold on a pan of simmering water. Steam for forty minutes. Loosen and place on heated plate. Serve.

Cheese Blintzes

Filling:
12 oz. unsalted Farmer's cheese
3 T Sugar
2 tsp fresh lemon juice
6 oz. whipped Cream cheese
6 T sour cream
¼ tsp salt

Batter:
1 cup white flour
2 T sugar
½ cup clarified butter
5 eggs, whole
1¼ cups cold water
1 tsp salt

Begin with the filling. Place all the ingredients in a bowl and mix thoroughly. When smooth, place in a bowl and set aside.

Place the flour, eggs, water, salt and sugar into a blender. Blend at a medium speed until *very* smooth. Remove to a bowl.

Heat the clarified butter and saute' blintzes on both Pour in enough batter to coat the bottom. Remove when the bottom is lightly browned. Stack until you've exhausted the batter supply.

Spoon out approximately 3 T of the filling on each pancake and roll carefully, tucking in the ends. Chill for an hour.

Heat the clarified butter and saute blintzes on both sides until brown. Serve.

Camembert Dessert

1 ripe Camembert cheese
1½ glasses white wine (approx.)
1/3 cup sweet butter
1 cup oven-toasted fine bread crumbs

Skin the cheese, cut into chunks with wine and let stand in the open air for 8-14 hours. Drain and dry the cheese. Place the cheese in a bowl and mix with the softened butter until creamy. With your hands, mold the cheese to its original shape and coat with crumbs. Chill for one hour and serve.

No-Bake Cheesecake

Filling:
- 3 cups beaten Cottage cheese
- 2 separated eggs
- 1 cup sugar
- 1 cup whipping cream
- 1 T lemon juice
- 1 tsp grated lemon/orange rind
- 1 tsp vanilla extract
- 2 T gelatin

Pie crust:
- ¾ cup crumbled Graham Crackers
- 2 T sugar
- ¼ tsp cinnamon
- ¼ tsp nutmeg
- 3 T melted sweet butter
- dash of salt

First—make the crust. Begin by mixing all your crust ingredients in a large bowl. Mold about ½ cup into a 9-inch pie plate. Refrigerate.

Begin the filling. Mix ¾ of your sugar, the gelatin and the salt in a bowl and set aside. Mix the egg yolks and mix together and blend into the sugar/gelatin mixture. Remove it to a pan and place over a low flame, stirring constantly to thicken the mixture. After it thickens, remove from the heat and add the lemon juice, rind and vanilla. Chill. Stir occasionally until mixture firms.

Beat the egg whites and remaining sugar together until smooth and stiff. Set aside. Beat the Cottage cheese until creamy and fold in the egg whites and gelatin mixture. Whip the cream and fold it into the mixture. Scoop into the pie plate and sprinkle with the remaining crumb mixture. Serve chilled and firm.

Plum Good Cream Cheese Pie

8 oz. softened Cream cheese
½ cup condensed milk
5 T softened butter
¼ tsp vanilla
1 cup sugar
⅛ tsp salt
1½ tsp cornstarch
½ cup chilled whipping cream
2 T fresh lemon juice
1½ tsp grated lemon peel
5 T sugar
1 lb halved cream
1 2/3 cup Graham Cracker Crumbs
¾ cup water
1 lb halved plums

Filling:
  In a bowl, place the softened cream cheese and slowly blend in the vanilla, milk, lemon juice and peel until smooth.
  In a chilled bowl, beat the chilled whipping cream with the chilled beaters. Fold the cream into the cheese mixture and chill.
Crust:
  Place the crumbs in a large bowl. Mix the salt and sugar into it. With a pastry knife, cut in the butter. Place in a pie pan and press evenly into sides and back.

Fill the crust with filling and chill.

Plum Good Glaze:

Over a low heat dissolve the sugar and water. Boil for 3-5 minutes. Add the plums and boil 1-2 minutes until tender. Remove and set aside. Heat the cornstarch and slowly blend in glaze; boil for three minutes. Remove from flame and allow to cool. Place plums on pie and pour on cooled glaze. Chill for one hour before serving.

Family Sized, Fast Cheese Trifle

16 oz. whipped Cream cheese
5 ladyfingers, sliced thin
1 pkg vanilla pudding mix
¼ cup sugar
2 envelopes plain gelatin
1 cup heavy cream-whipped
2 T sherry
2 cups milk
2 egg whites
2 egg yolks
9 oz. crushed pineapple

Lay the sliced ladyfingers flat and sprinkle with sherry. Butter an 8-inch bowl and line the sides and bottom with the ladyfingers.

Dump the pudding mix and gelatin in a pan; add milk and eggs. Beat until blended. Place over a flame, slowly raising the heat while stirring constantly until it reaches a boil. Remove and add to a bowl the Cream cheese and the pineapple. Chill, stirring occasionally until the mixture puffs.

Beat the egg whites and sugar to form a meringue

and then fold the meringue in the mixture. Then fold in the whipped cream. Pour the mixture into the pan over the lady fingers. Refrigerate for at least 5 hours before serving.

Cheese Crust

1 cup finely grated mild Cheddar cheese
¼ cup melted butter
½ tsp salt
¾ cup fine white flour
¼ tsp dry English mustard

Mix all the ingredients together in a bowl with a pastry blender until smooth. Knead the mixture for about one minute. The dough is now ready to be pressed into the bottom and sides of a greased 9 inch pie plate. The crust is especially good with vegetable or meat pies.

Russian Cheese Pashka

3 cups Cottage cheese
2 egg yolks
½ cup sugar
4 T softened un-salted butter
1 cup whipping cream
½ cup chopped almonds
1/3 cup chopped candied fruit

Force the Cottage cheese through a food sieve.

Place in a bowl with softened butter and mix well. Set aside.

Place the whipping cream in a pan and bring just to the point of boiling. Remove from the heat and set aside.

Mix the egg yolks and sugar and heat with an electric mixer for 2-3 minutes. Slowly add the whipping cream and then place over a low flame until it thickens. Stir constantly. Remove and mix in the fruits and nuts, and transfer to a bowl. Set the bowl inside another bowl filled with ice and stir until chilled. Once chilled, add the Cottage cheese mixture. Refrigerate for eight hours and serve.

Ricotta Indian Dessert

3½ cups Ricotta cheese
½ tsp ground cardamom
1½ cups powdered sugar

Cream the Ricotta until smooth and place in a pan. Slowly add the powdered sugar, mixing thoroughly. Heat until the mixture leaves the pan's sides. Add the cardamom and remove from the heat. While the mixture is still hot, roll into small balls. Chill for 15 minutes and serve.

Sauces
&
Frostings

Mornay Sauce

½ cup grated Parmesan cheese
½ cup grated Swiss cheese
½ onion
¾ cup chicken broth
¾ cup half and half
3 T white flour
3 T sweet butter
½ tsp salt
⅛ tsp white pepper

In a saucepan, melt the butter and remove from the flame. Mix in salt, pepper and flour. Slowly add the broth. Mix well. Slowly add the cream and mix well. Drop the onion in, in one solid piece. Return to the low flame and allow to thicken, stirring constantly until smooth, for 4-5 minutes. Remove the onion and slowly add the cheeses. Stir continually for two more minutes.

Cottage Cheese Sauce (especially good on any fruit)

1 cup Cottage cheese
2 T powdered sugar
1/3 cup evaporated milk
½ tsp vanilla extract

Mix the Cottage cheese, vanilla, milk and sugar in a blender until smooth and fluffy. Remove and refrigerate until needed.

Tomato/Cheese Sauce (for meats and Fish)

1 cup shredded Cheddar cheese
2 cups tomato juice
1 mashed bouillon cube
3 T white flour
3 T butter
½ tsp salt
dash of black pepper

Melt the butter and remove the pan from the flame. Slowly blend in the salt, flour and pepper into it. Mix well. Slowly add the tomato juice and mix well. Add the bouillon. Return the pan to the flame until it thickens, stirring constantly for 4-5 minutes. Slowly add the cheese and continue stirring. Cook two more minutes and remove.

Quicky Cheese Sauce

2 cups grated American processed cheese
½ cup milk
pinch of white pepper

In the top of a double boiler, melt the cheese. While stirring, add milk and pepper. Great over all vegetables.

Cream Cheese Frosting

¾ cup Cream cheese
¼ cup Cottage cheese
2 tsp sour cream
1 egg white
3 T powdered sugar
cream to thin

Place all ingredients in a bowl except sugar and cream. Whip with an electric mixer until smooth. Thin slightly and add the powdered sugar until sweet enough. Whip until smooth and blended. Makes about 1½ cups. If a sauce for fruit is desired, add less sugar and thin with cream to pouring consistency.